SCRAPYARD ARMOUR

MODELLING SCENES FROM A RUSSIAN ARMOUR SCRAPYARD

Rows and rows of old tanks taken out of service, lined up and waiting to be cut up for scrap. Others have already had their turrets tipped off and have been torch-cut into three pieces causing their nose and tails to droop like decaying animal carcasses. Elsewhere a complete T54 stands amid the weeds, its turret numbers fading as it slowly corrodes.

The scrapyard offers a unique set of challenges for the armour modeller with faded and peeling paint, stripped out vehicles, cut up turrets and of course plenty of rust. We found inspiration in a series of photographs of one such scrapyard which we brought together here along with the models they inspired, in the hope that they will inspire you too to take up the challenge of Scrapyard Armour.

TRISECTED T-62

Modelled by David Parker

TRISECTED T-62

I dont think I had ever seen images of a tank chopped up like this before and I was immediately intrigued. The tilted nose with its empty ammunition bins and the discarded turret offered a very different challenge. At first glance the interior of the T-62 seemed very similar to that of the CMK T-55 interior detail set that I had tucked away and Trumpeter's T-62 kits offered the basis to realise the vehicle from the scrapyard.

I quickly realised that the interior of a T-55 and T-62 although similar are different enough to render the interior set virtually useless apart from a few small parts. Before long the project had grown into an immensely complex scratchbuilding task before moving on to be an immensely complex painting project.

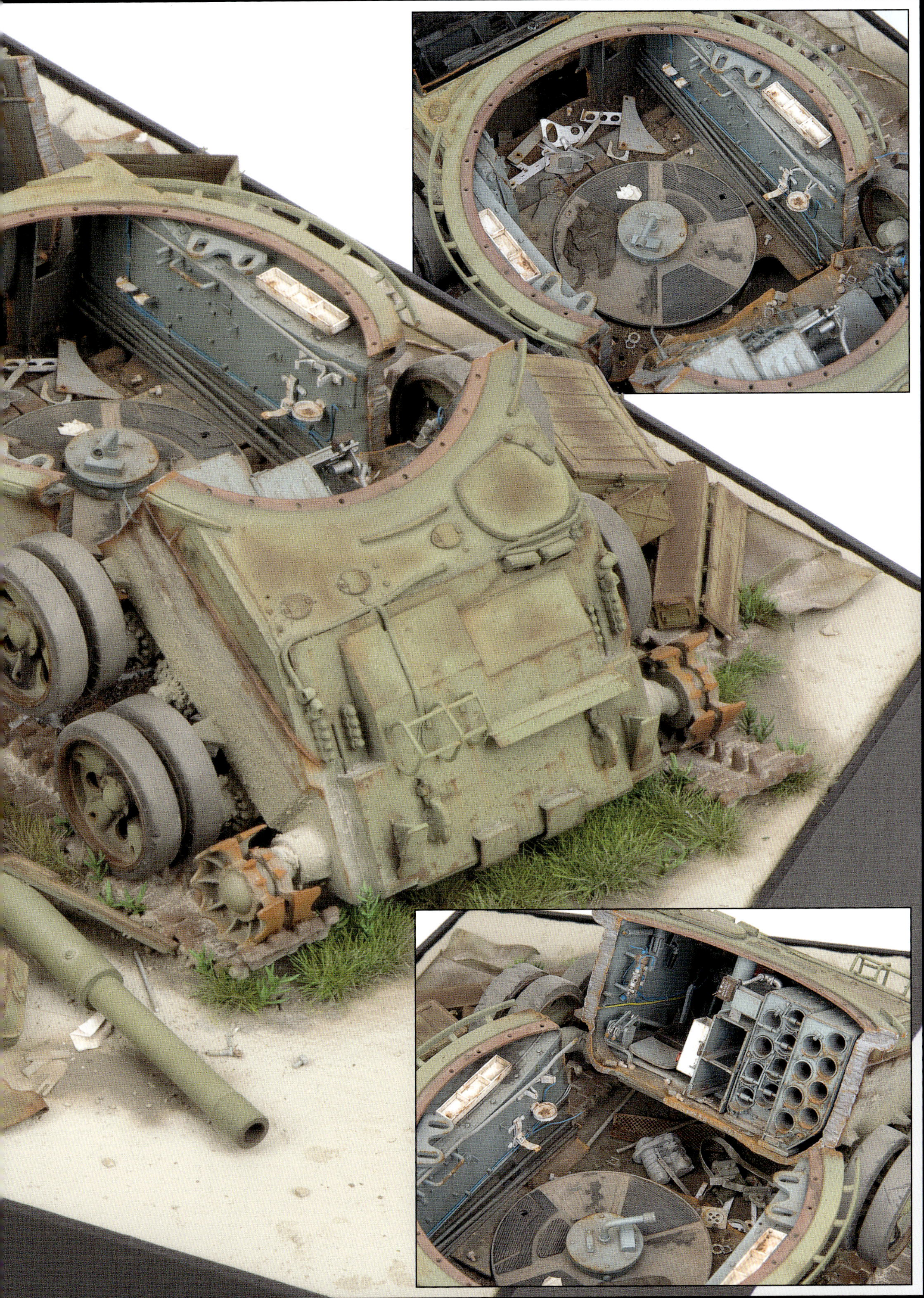

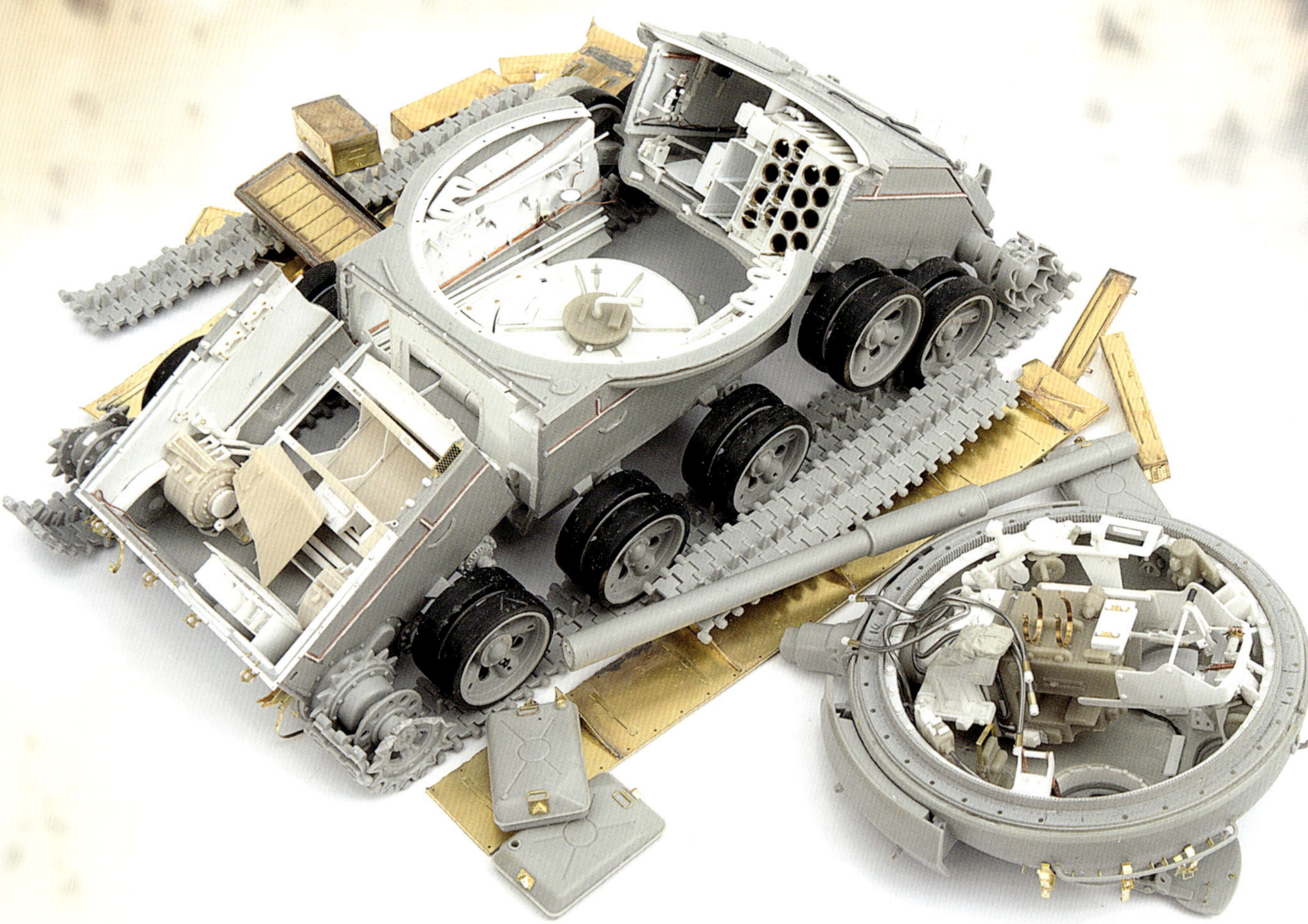

Work begins on the turret to build up the thickness of the armour from the thin plastic shell. I added a pair of plastic rings to each hatch opening and began to add Magic Sculp in stages, building up the thickness.

One of the hatches has a small lip around it which was sculpted into the Magic Sculp and here the thicker cheek armour is being added and shaped.

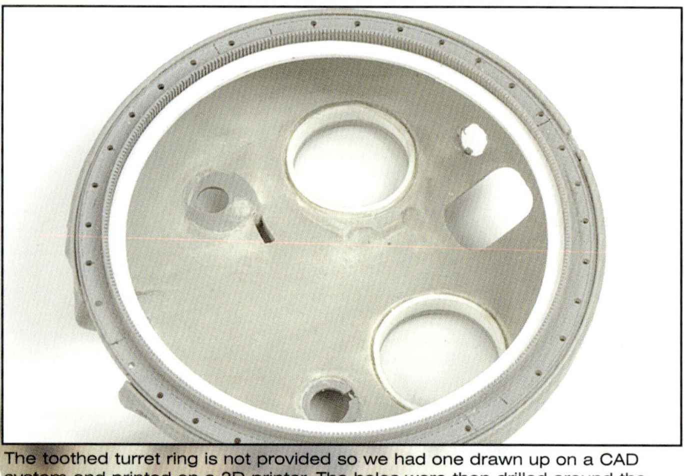

The toothed turret ring is not provided so we had one drawn up on a CAD system and printed on a 3D printer. The holes were then drilled around the edge and an inner ring cut from plastic card.

With the ring removed you can see the varying thicknesses of the turret and the lip on which the turret ring sits.

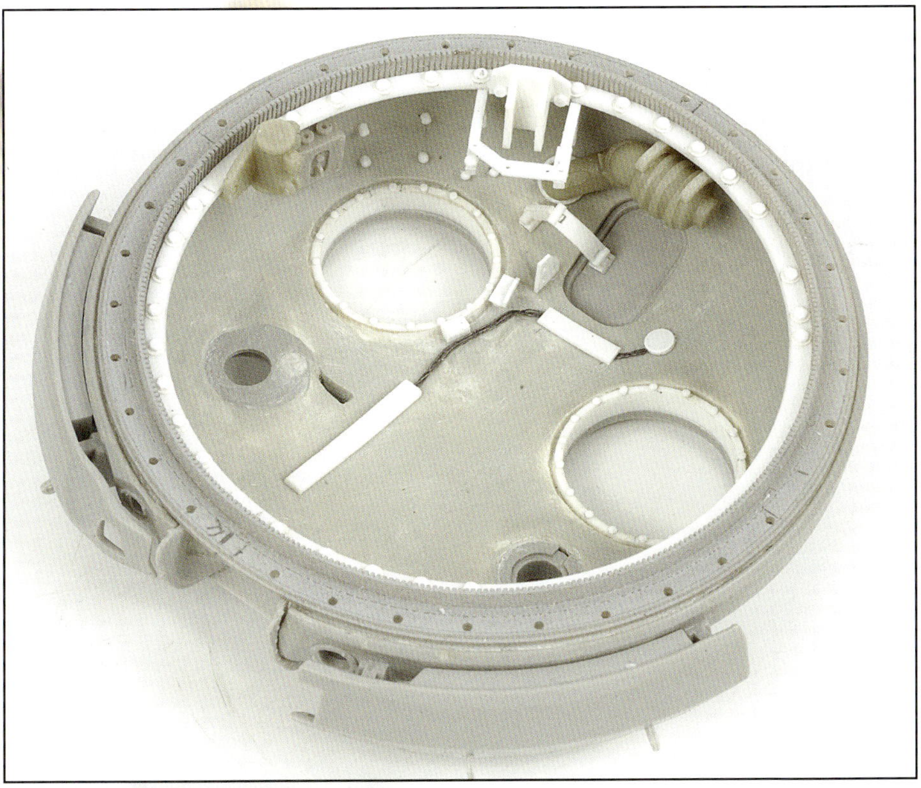

I purchased the Verlinden Productions T-62 interior set designed for the old Tamiya kit in the hope that it would provide some parts or at least visual guidance for me. In the end I only used the breech and a few parts like the pericopes to detail the turret. Here you can see a couple of the grey-green Verlinden resin parts installed along with the hinge mechanism for the shell ejector door. Wiring on the turret roof has been added along with some mounting lugs on the back wall. I have also started adding bolt head and washer detail to the inner turret ring but the ring remains a separate piece throughout construction to make it easier to work inside the turret.

Below work begins on the massive breech of the gun and here the Verlinden set came to the rescue by providing the majority of the breech which would have been a complex item to build from scratch. I had to cut down the front of the breech to add the correct intersection between the breech and the gun barrel which then had to be married to the kit mantlet parts. I also drilled out a cavity in the bottom of the breech to allow me to mount the pair of recuperator cylinders which were missing from the Verlinden part.

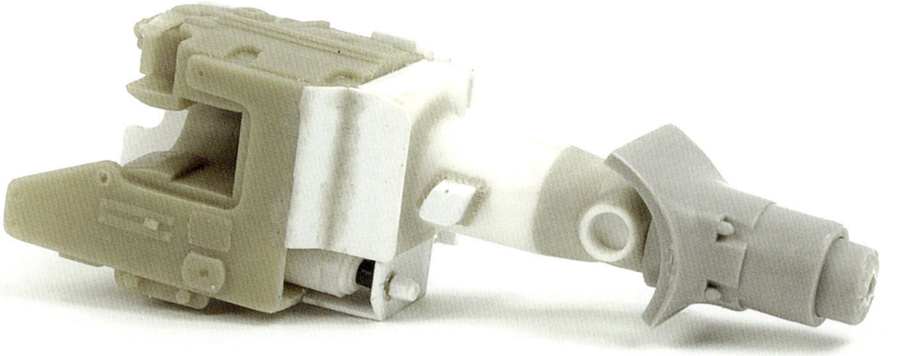

New breech guards were assembled from plastic card and the elevation gears were also added to the left hand side.

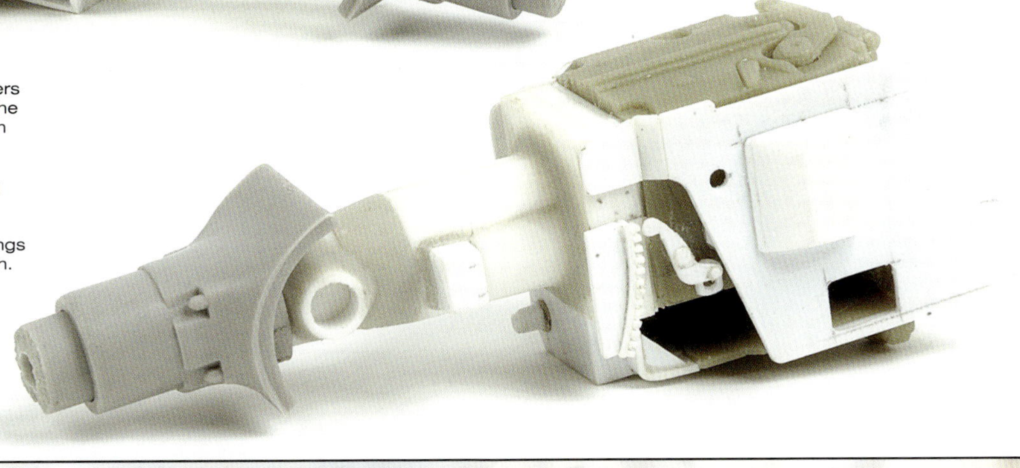

One of the recuperator cylinders can be seen here fitted in to the new opening under the breech

Magic Sculp is great for doing the smooth blends between parts like those on the gun barrel. The pair of circular fittings are the pivot points for the gun.

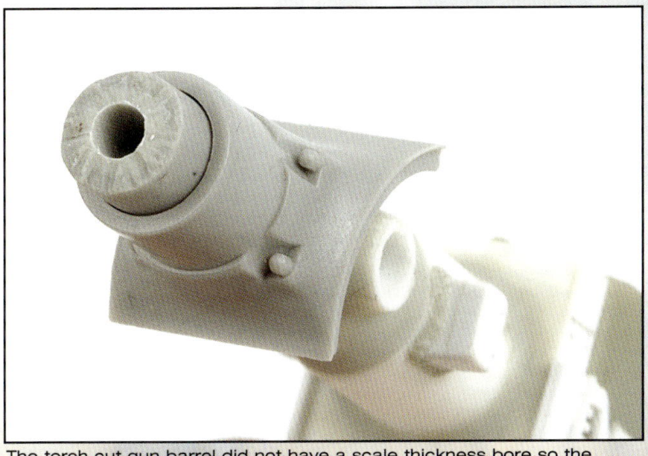

The torch cut gun barrel did not have a scale thickness bore so the centre was filled out with Magic Sculp and the torched cut lines were sculpted into in before it hardened.

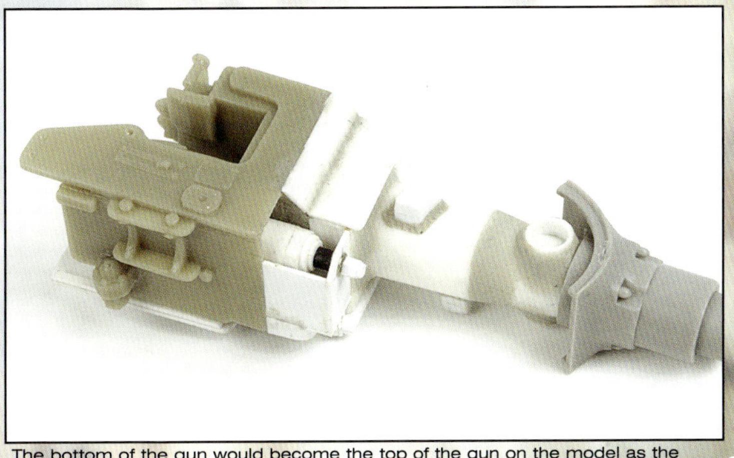

The bottom of the gun would become the top of the gun on the model as the turret is upturned so it was important to keep this side neat and tidy.

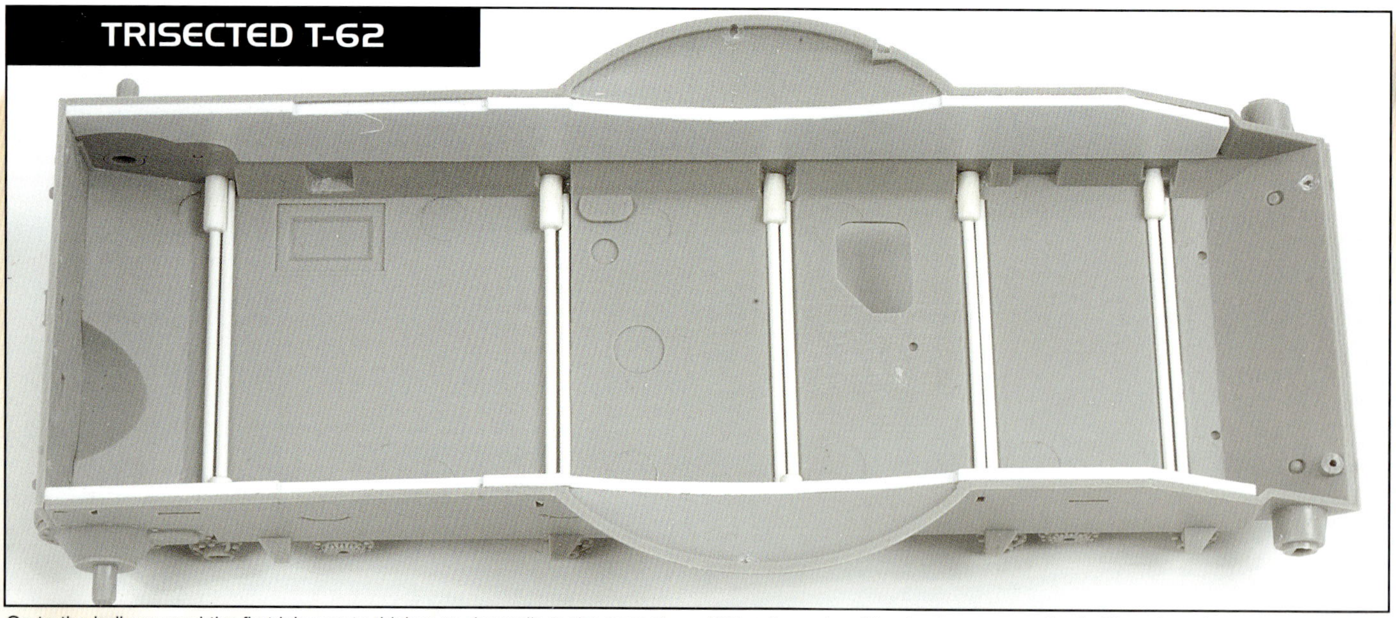

On to the hull now and the first job was to thicken up the walls to the correct scale thickness which was done with sheets of plastic card. Fortunately the angled walls and floor were the right thickness so these were unmodified.

Fitting the pairs of torsion bars across the hull into the rebates for them in the floor required a bit of cheating to get them all to fit but the finished result does the job.

Before cutting up the hull I had to add the remains of the trackguards which had been cut off. I used plastic card to add a 2mm deep section of trackguard and ribs.

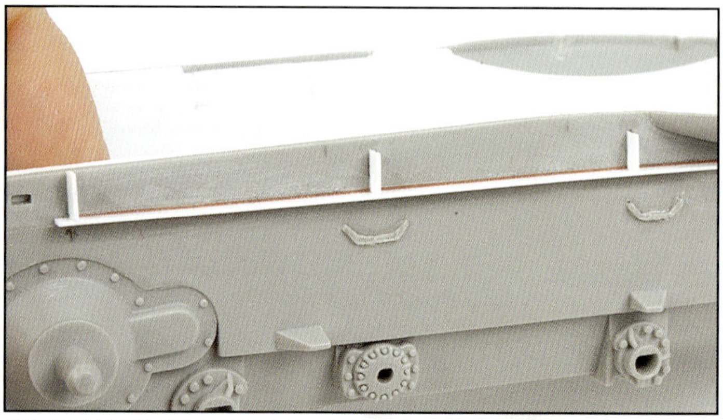

Thin (red) plastic rod was then glued along these to form the weld beads and they were generously painted with liquid glue which causes the rod to distort into a convincing weld texture.

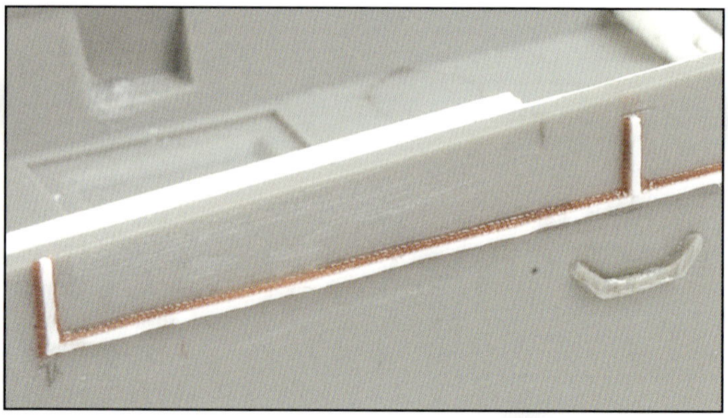

When this was all dry I used a scalpel to shave off the excess plastic strip until a small lip remained and this was deliberately given an uneven bumpy finish.

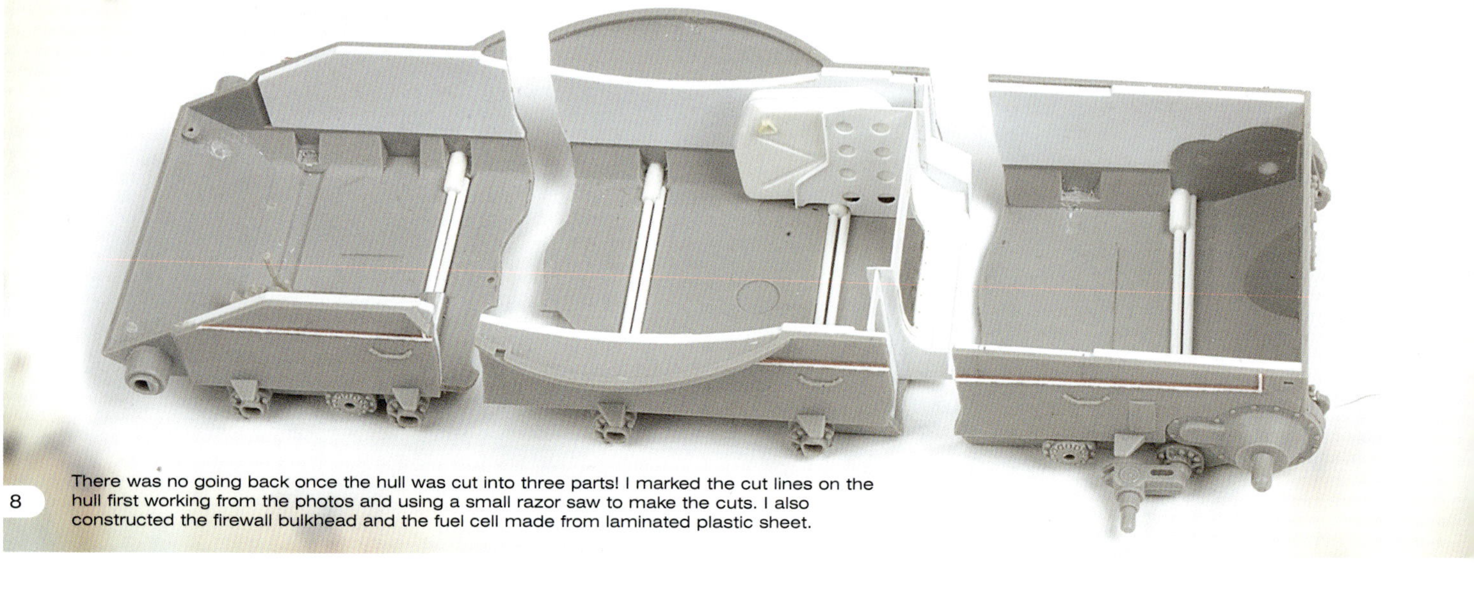

There was no going back once the hull was cut into three parts! I marked the cut lines on the hull first working from the photos and using a small razor saw to make the cuts. I also constructed the firewall bulkhead and the fuel cell made from laminated plastic sheet.

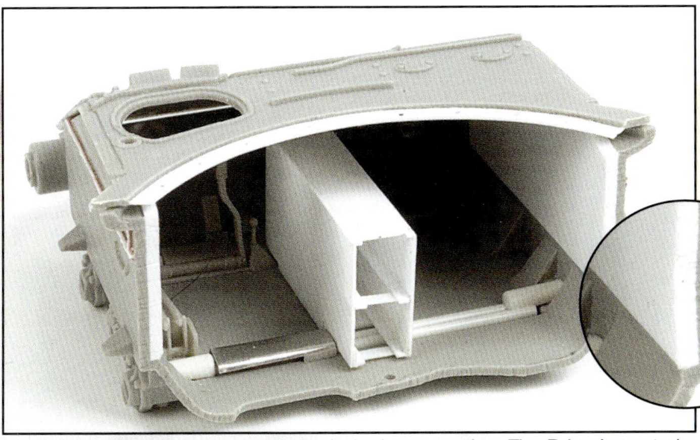

The hull roof was also cut up to match the lower section. The Driver's controls were taken from the CMK T-55 interior set and the central battery box was constructed from plastic. Pewter sheet was used for the torsion bar cover.

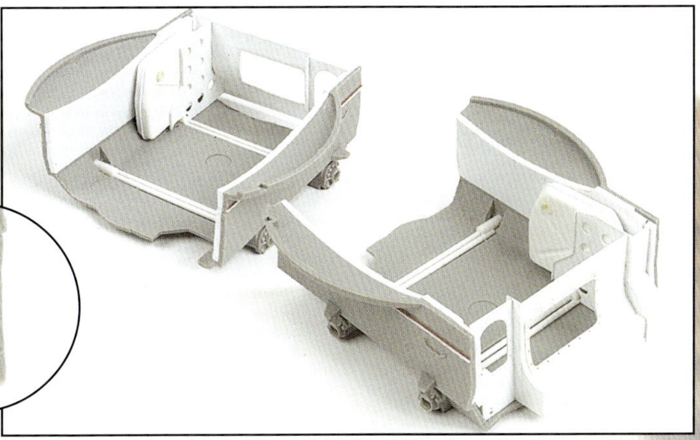

The central section with the firewall dry fitted. The firewall overhangs the cut line but I left it intact at this stage. The torch-cut edges of the hull were textured with a file to give the irregular surface.

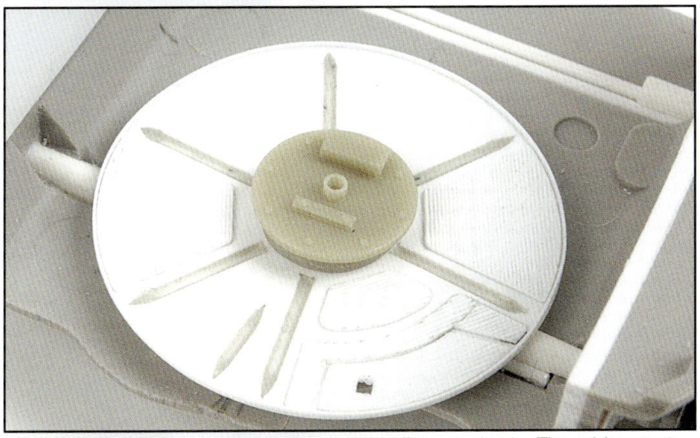

The turret floor was almost entirely scratchbuilt from plastic. The rubber mat segments were cut to shape and then engraved with parallel lines using a P Cutter. The rebated ribs were cut as slots and blanked off with a backing panel. Magic Sculp was then forced into the slots and smoothed off with a suitably sized round tip. The centre hub comes from the Verlinden interior set.

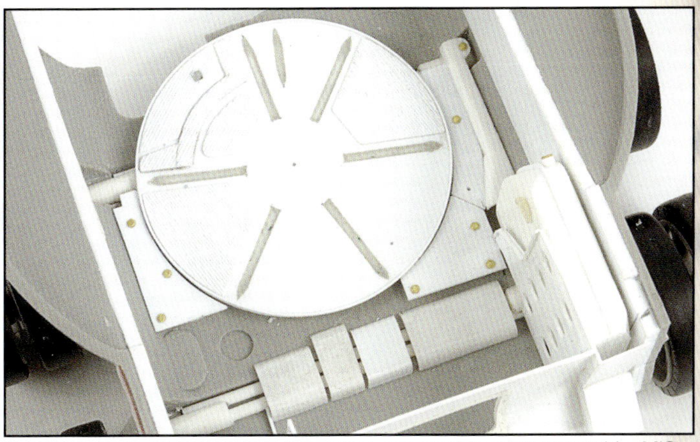

Next I began to add the floor panels which surround the turret turntable. MIG Productions etched bolts were used to add the fixings and thin plastic sheet was used to make the covers for the torsion bars.

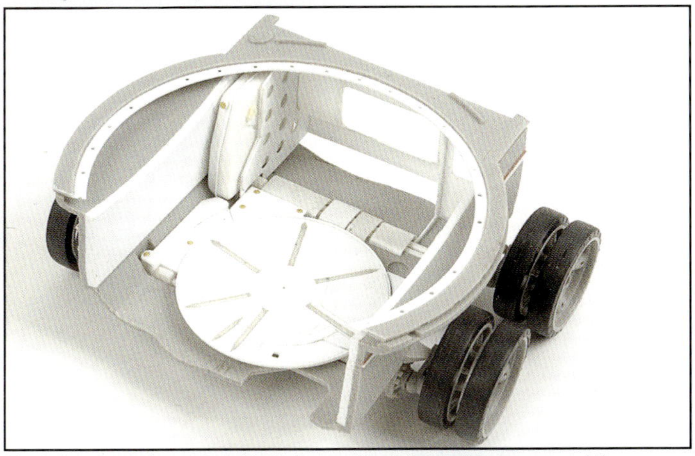

The inner turret ring was added along with all the bolt holes around the circumference and you can see that the hull floor escape hatch has been cut out.

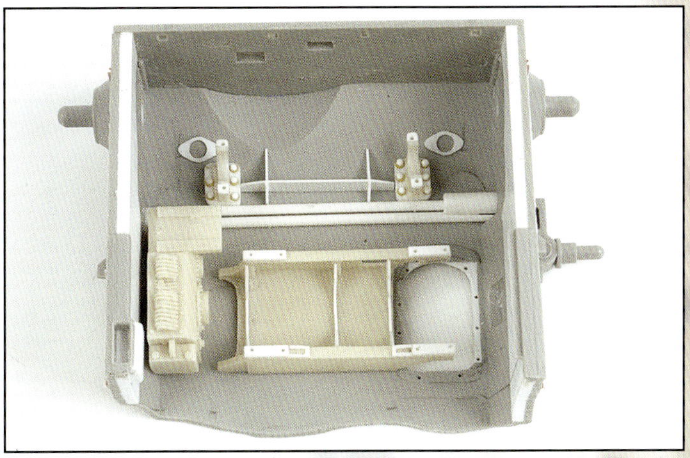

In the engine bay the floor inspection hatch was opened and modified to the correct shape. The CMK T-55 Interior detail set provided the resin parts here with additional detail added to the engine frame.

Test fitting is extremely important and here are the three section of the hull with wheels temporarily mounted to check the overall composition.

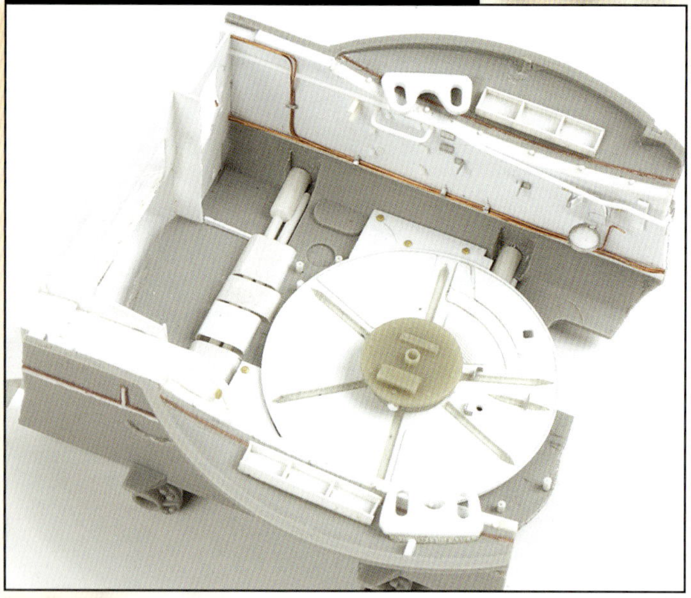
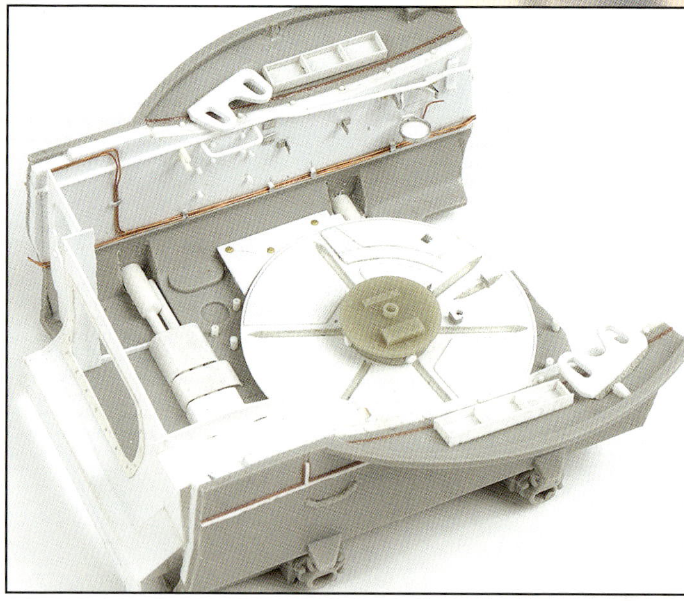

I moved on to detailing the side walls of the centre section, working from the photos. Fine copper electrical wire was used to add the cabling and some of the smaller clips and brackets were added from metal foil. The weld lines along the extended turret wings were added with fine plastic rod in the same way as those on the remains of the trackguards.

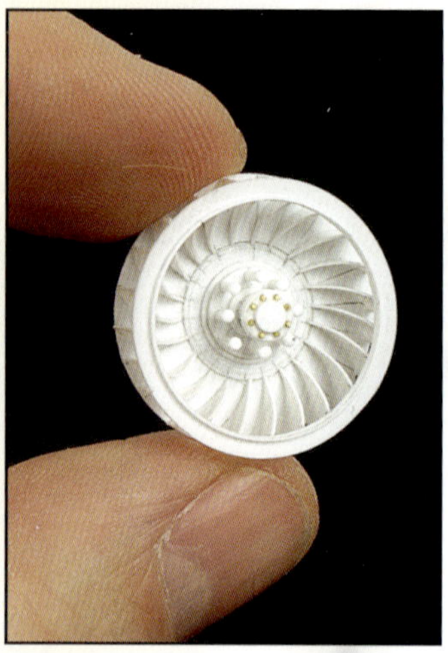

The next challenge was the construction of the distinctive cooling fan for the engine bay. It looks more complex than it is as long as you break down the assembly. I cut circles of plastic for the back plate and front rings and then I marked out the divisions for the position of the fan blades. After some trial and error I worked out the shape of an individual blade before using this as a template to cut out multiple copies. These were then given a curve by pulling them over a hard edge. The blades were then fitted to the backing ring carefully following the marked out spacings. With the blades in position the front rings could be dropped into place and carefully aligned. The final task was to add the hub details. With the fan assembled I was then able to build the remains of the fan housing which had been partly stripped out on the subject vehicles.

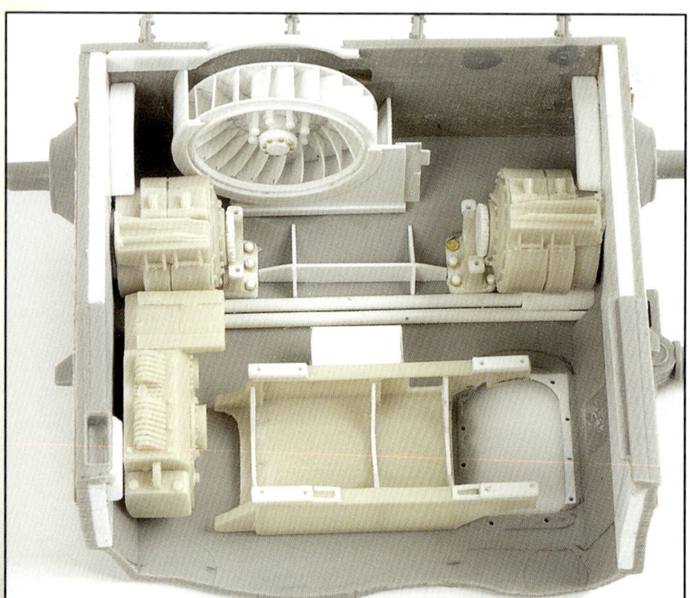
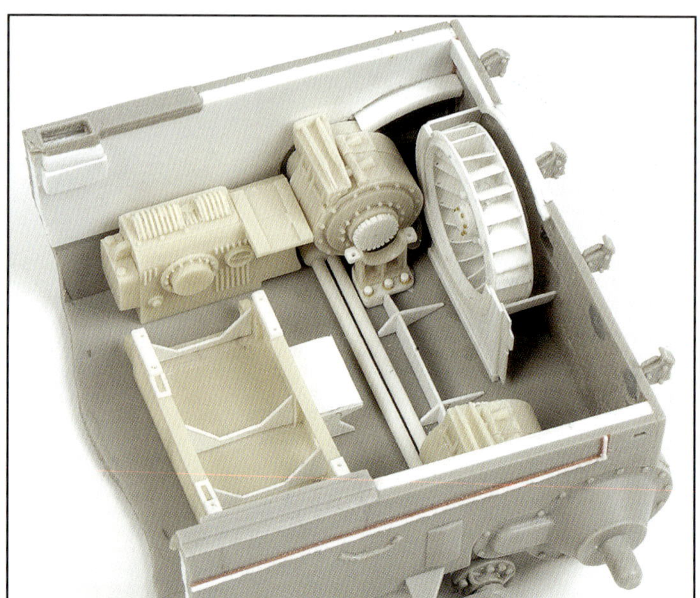

The other components of the engine bay are test fitted again and the pair of steering brakes were fitted, which have again been modified from the CMK set. With the gearbox removed I had to add the gear wheels on the outer face of the brakes.

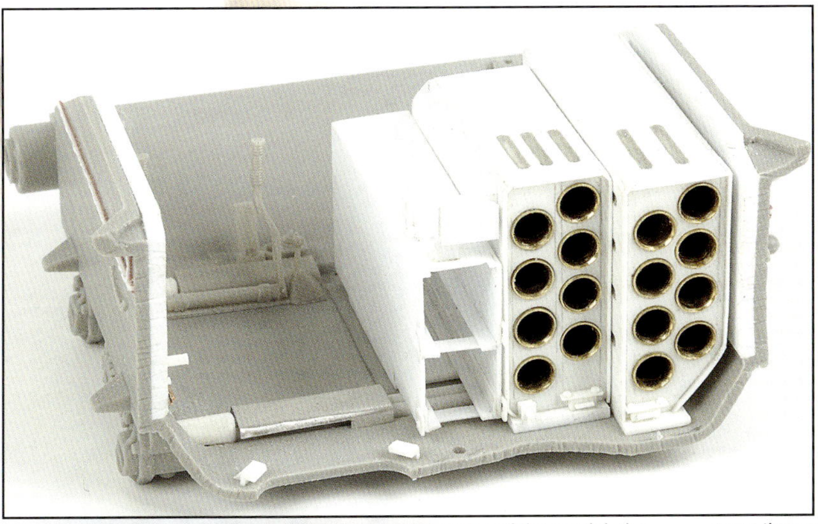

Back to the bow again and one of the most visible parts of the model, the combined ammunition rack/fuel tanks. These utilise the space around the tubes that hold the shells to carry fuel in a rather scary combination. I began by cutting out the front face of the box structures and marking the position of the tubes. I used Albion Alloys brass tube which I cut into lengths and I thinned the edges of the open ends for a more scale appearance. The tubes were then glued into the face plates and the rest of the boxes were then constructed around these. The recessed ribs were added with Magic Sculp in the same way was as those in the turret turntable. The assorted clasps and lips on the front of racks were added from plastic and fine Albion Alloys brass tube. Happily the right hand rack has had most of these details torched off so I only had to add the remains of these details.

I also added the third fuel cell that sits right in the nose, it is not very visible but leaving a big hole instead is very visible!

Up on its wheels, the nose is beginning to look the part now with the Driver's seat from the CMK T-55 kit (with a new seat back) in place. The tread pattern on the kit wheels was sanded down for a smooth worn look.

Bringing the various parts together is essential to keep checking that if all works and that the model is capturing the look of the real thing. Leaving sub-assemblies separate also helps with access and if anything goes wrong you don't not have to strip back everything to fix it.

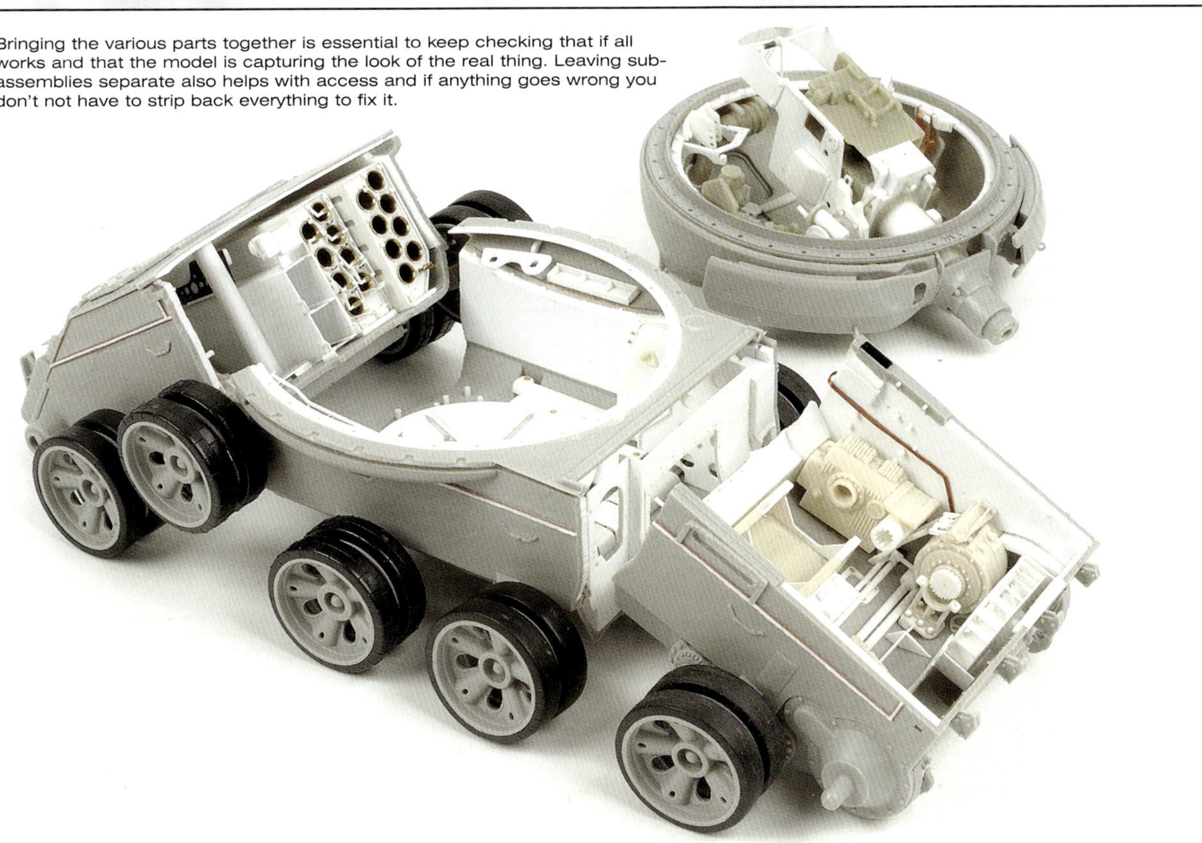

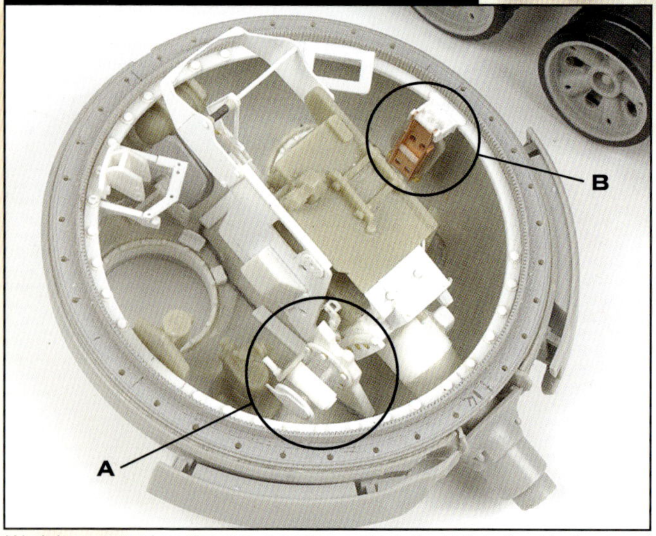

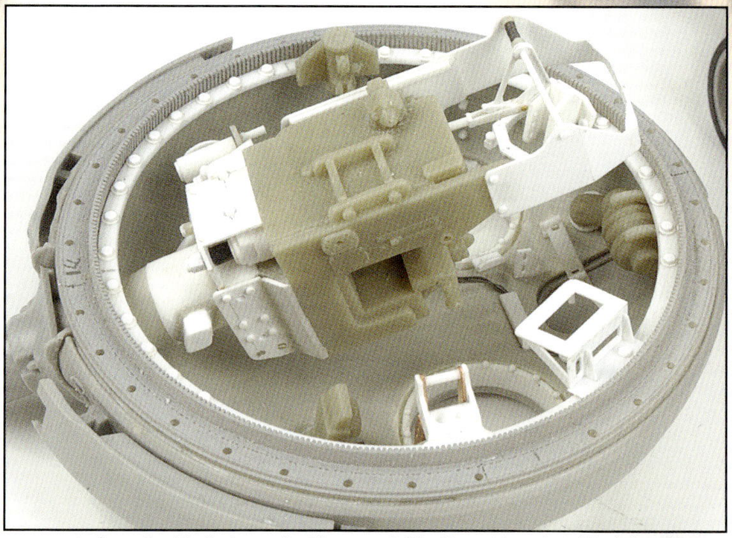

Work has started on the gun elevation system **A** which is fixed to the turret roof but just dry fitted here. The folded loader's seat **B** uses photoetched parts from the Verlinden set with a scratchbuilt seat bracket. Work has also started on the recoil guards for the breech.

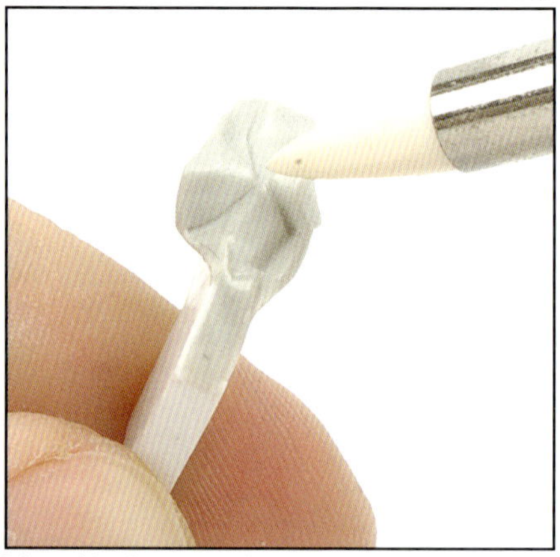

The spent ammunition collection bin for the co-axial MG is a thin sheet metal structure with a fabric pouch at the base. In the photos it has been crushed during the scrapping. To replicate this the basic shape was constructed in plastic and the damaged area formed with Magic Sculp. A rubber tipped brush is then used to distort it and create the creased areas of damage. This was allowed to harden and then the fabric bag was added along with the zip fastening.

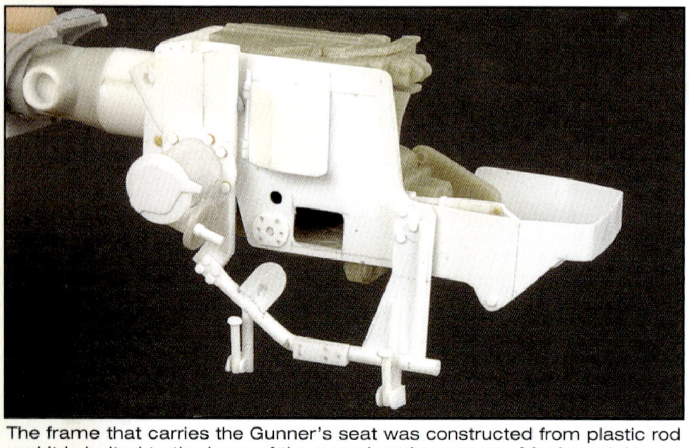

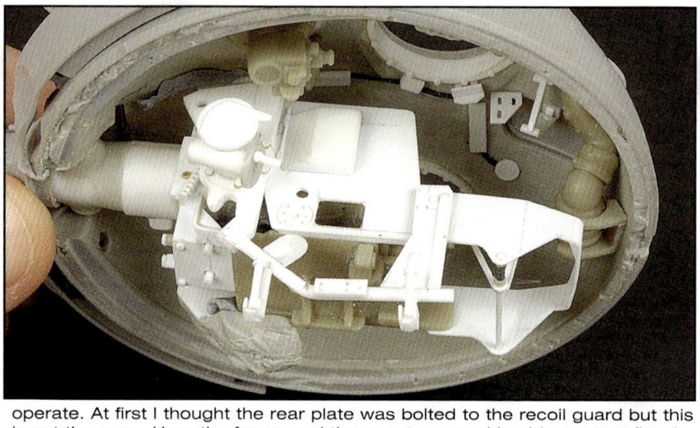

The frame that carries the Gunner's seat was constructed from plastic rod and it is bolted to the base of the gun elevation system. Much work is required with parts like these to understand how they look and also how they operate. At first I thought the rear plate was bolted to the recoil guard but this is not the case. Here the frame and the spent ammunition bin are test fitted into the turret.

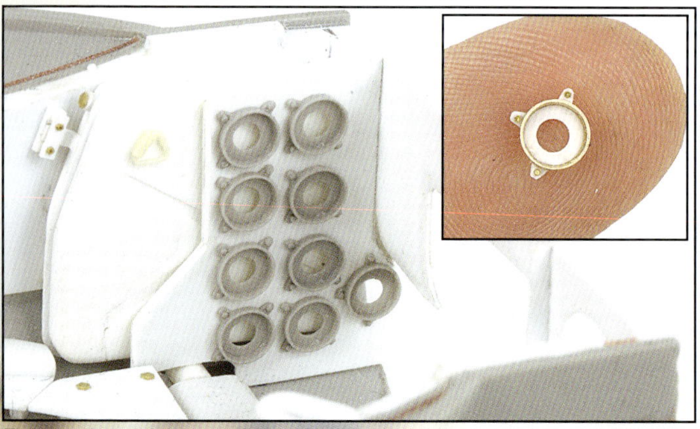

The remains of the ammunition racks on the hull firewall feature a number of identical brackets so I made a master bracket and had resin copies made.

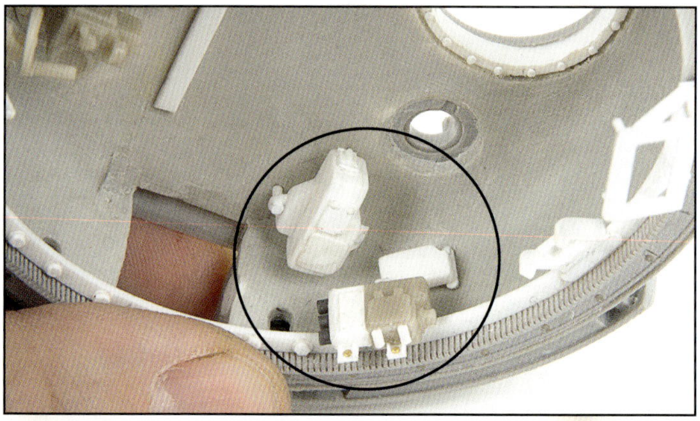

Further components are added inside the turret including the roof mounted hydraulic pump? Working without any drawings means that all the parts must be constantly test fitted.

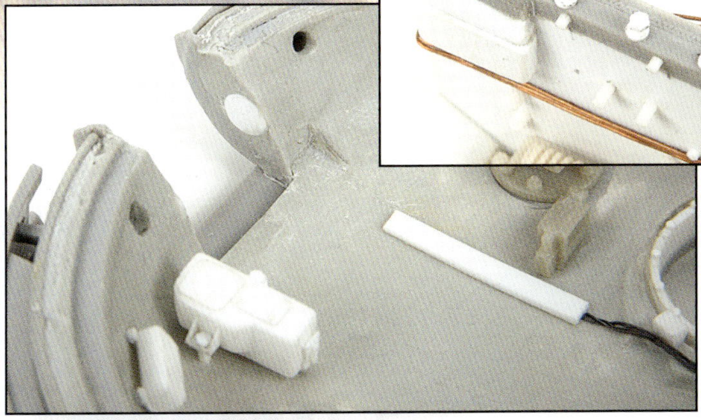

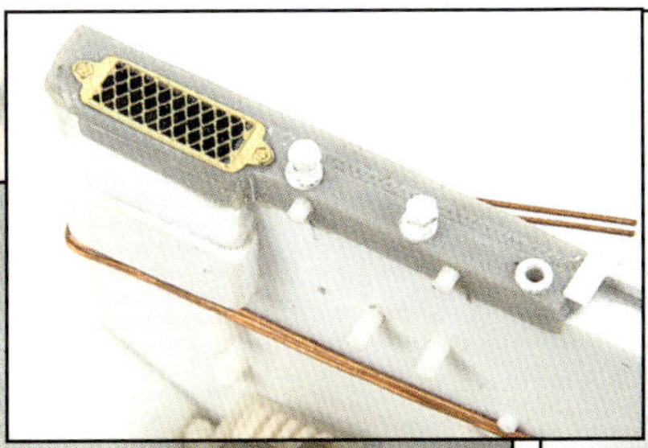

I finalised the opening for the gun mounting adding two plastic discs, one each side of the opening to marry with the mounting point on the gun barrel. The surrounding area was then build up using Magic Sculp for a neat finish. The small cut out in the roof is to seat the gun elevation system and Gunner's seat frame.

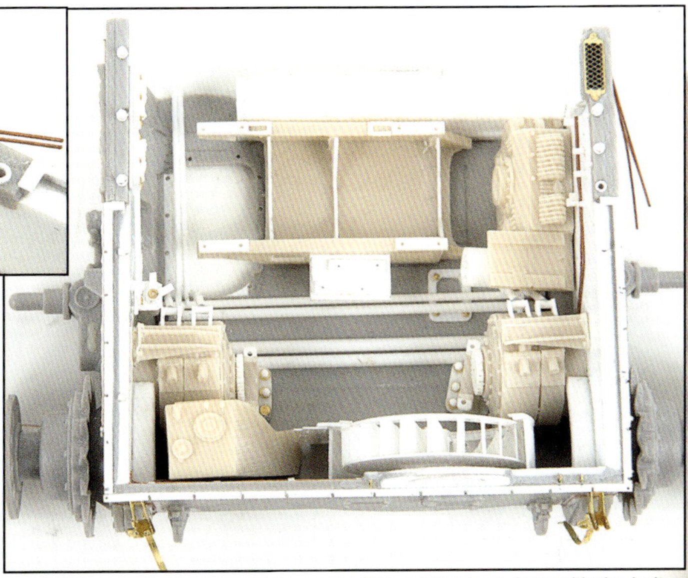

I added the small rails around the edge of the engine bay along with the bolt details. The small photoetched grille comes from the ET Models update set for the T-62.

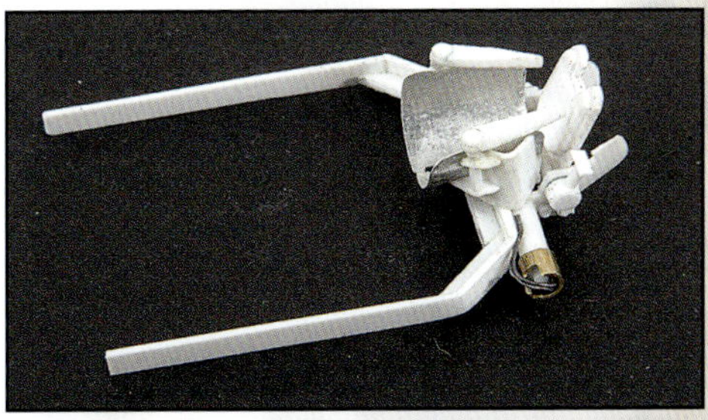

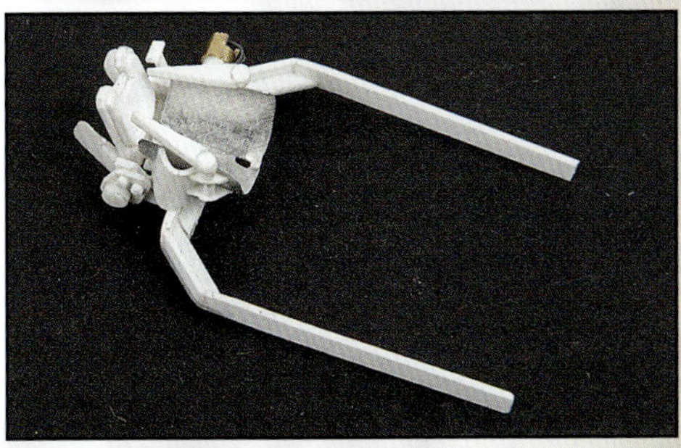

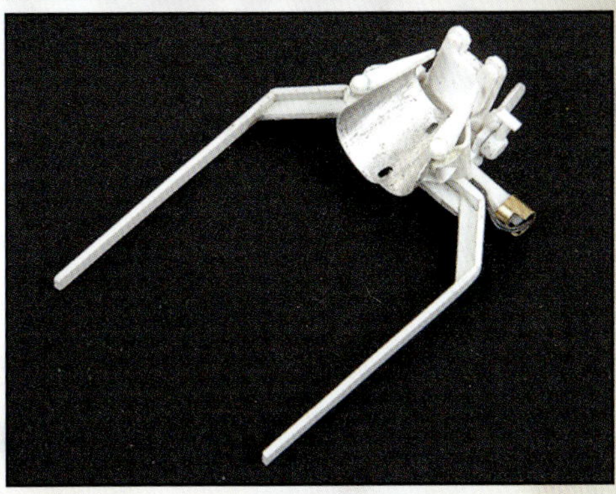

Right Without doubt one of the most complex parts of the whole build was the ejection mechanism for the gun. It was something that I had been putting off and took me quite some time to get an understanding of how it went together by comparing various photographs and diagrams from the vehicle's maintenance manuals. I began by making the tray from metal foil and then constructing the cradle that supports it. The angled frame was sized from its location on the breech. I had to also remember that the finished ejector would be seen from underneath so detail had to extend to the underside too.

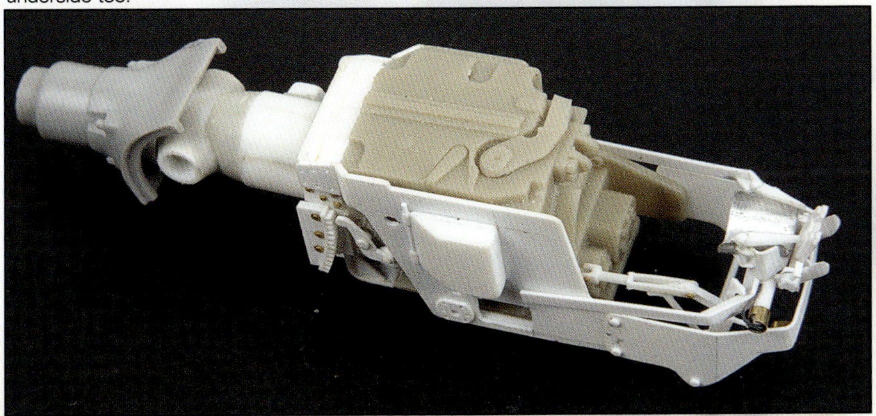

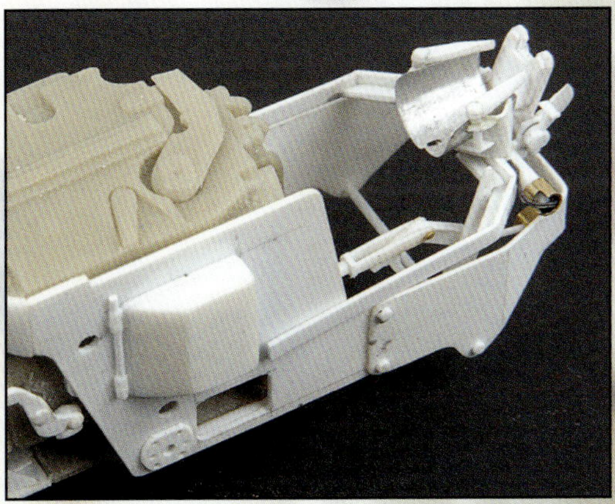

Here the ejector system is test fitted into position on the recoil guard rails, it still needs to have the springs and activation rods added to the underside.

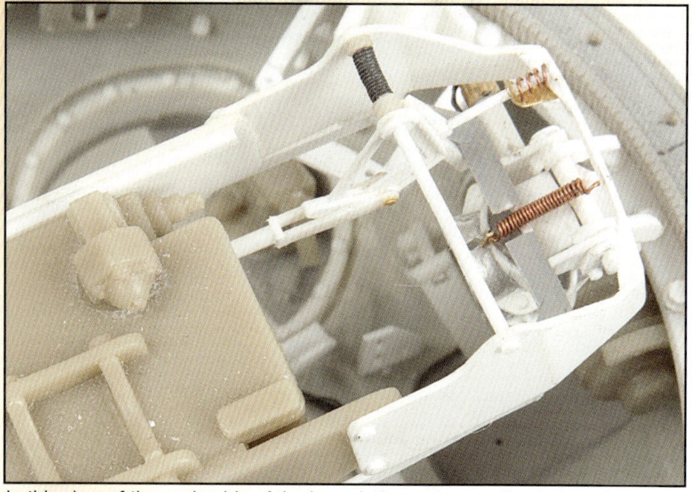

In this view of the underside of the breech the springs and rods have been added to the ejector system making for a very complex assembly which I was relieved to have finally completed.

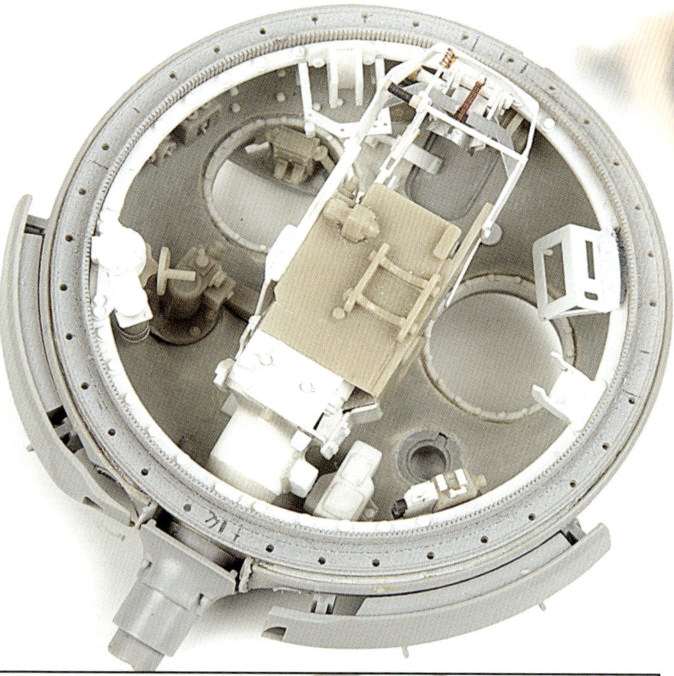

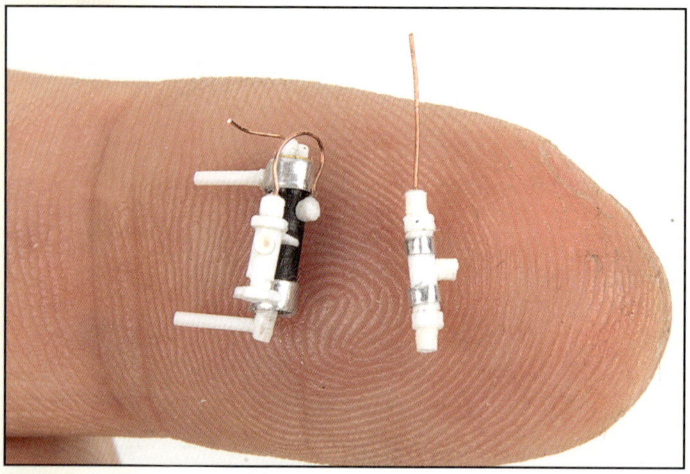

These tiny valves are part of the compressed air system in the vehicle and are prominently located on the side of the hull right next to the cut in the bow. I used different sized rods and adhesive aluminium foil to construct them.

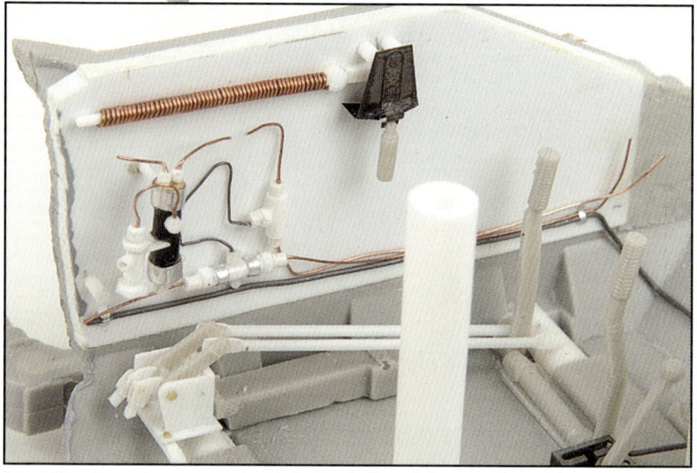

Here they have been mounted into the hull and the remains of the pipework have been added. The partly dismantled condition of the vehicle meant that I did not need to worry about replicating all the pipework exactly.

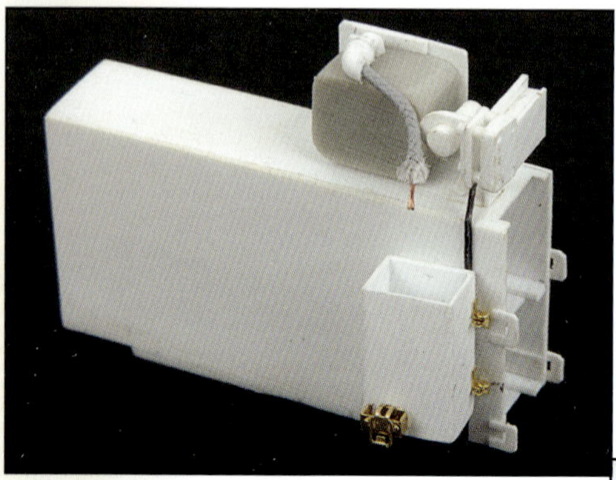

Additional details to the battery racks with brass brackets made from spare photoetched parts and a nylon chord used to make the frayed electrical cable complete with copper wires.

Right All the parts are dry fitted into the bow to make sure they all still fit and to see if it looks like the photos of the real thing

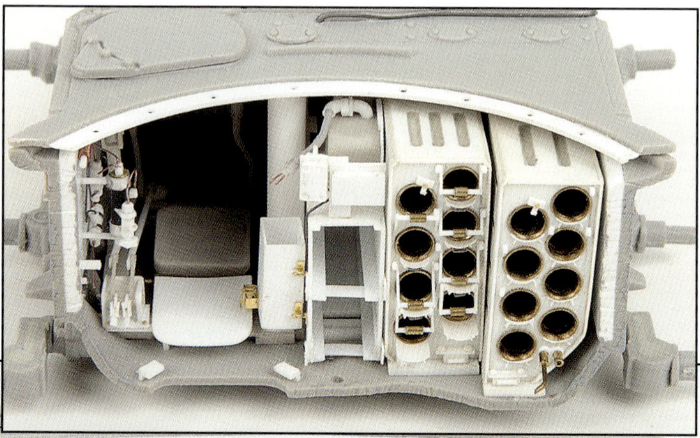

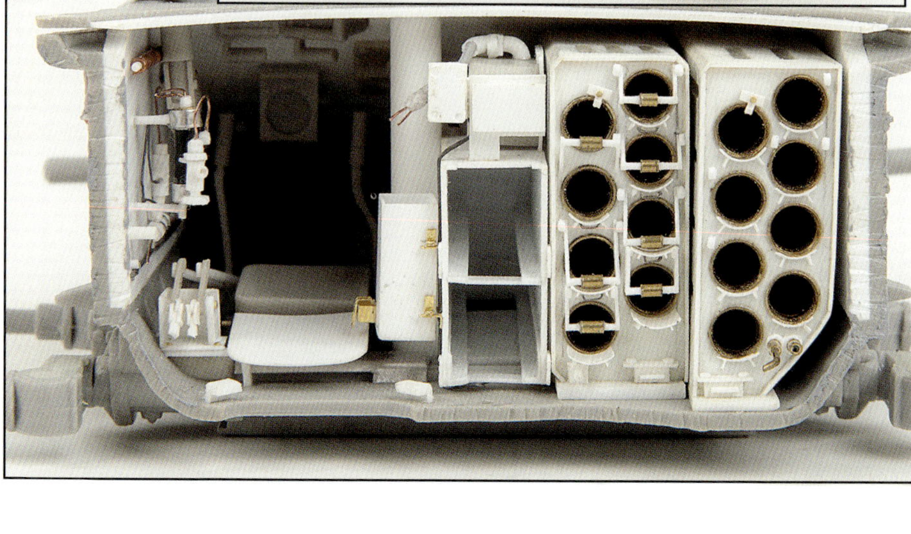

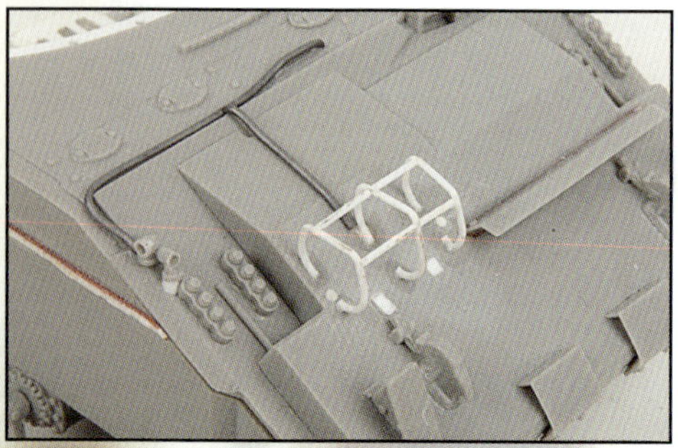

Externally I had to make a new headlamp guard frame from plastic rod , I drilled out the small convoy lights and added new cable conduits with lead wire.

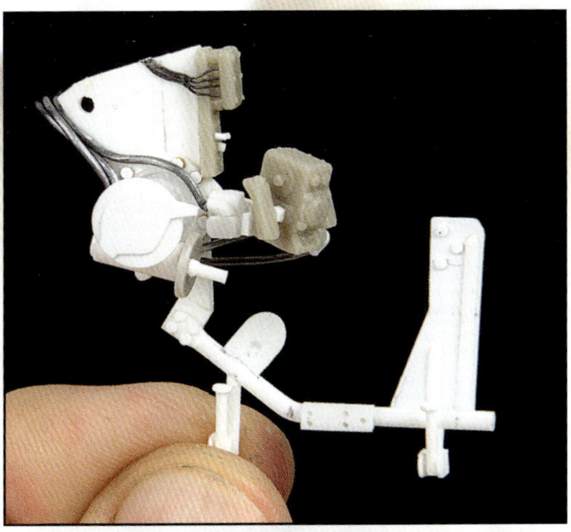

Final touches are added to the gunner's seat frame arrangement with the control grip and electrical panel pinched from the Verlinden T-62 interior set. The angled position of the control yoke required quite a bit of trial and error to set up. Lead wire cables were the final details to be added.

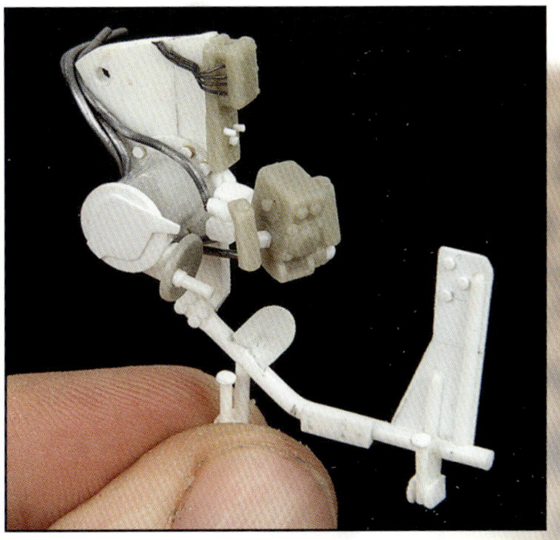

Below counterbalance weight plates are bolted to the base of the breech and I made the brass straps using off cuts from photoetch frets.

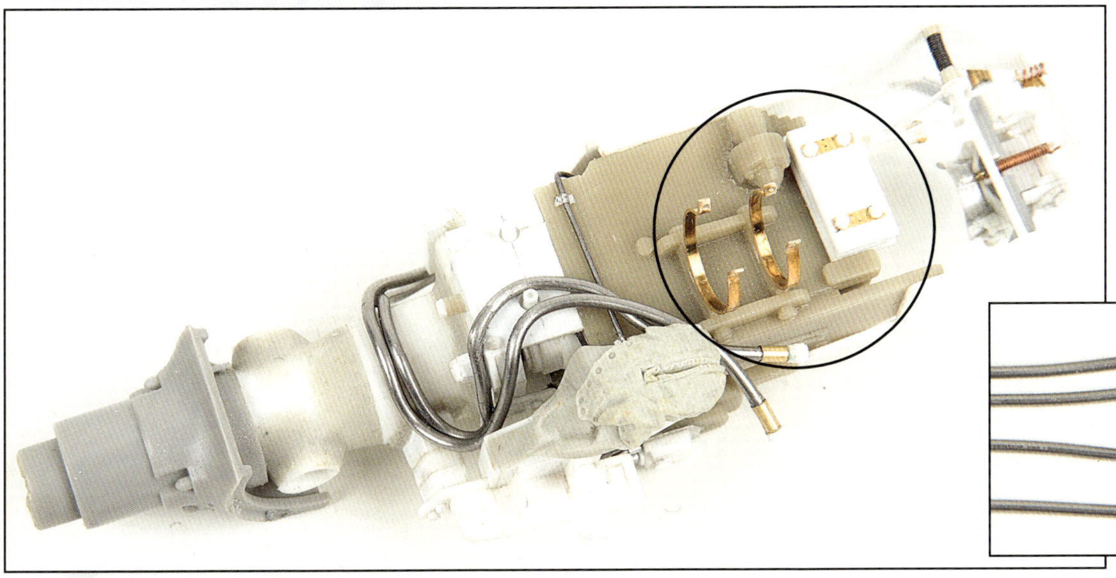

The disconnected hydraulic hoses are best made from lead wire again to help get a realistic drape. A brass tube collar and plastic bolt head and washer were added to each end of the hoses.

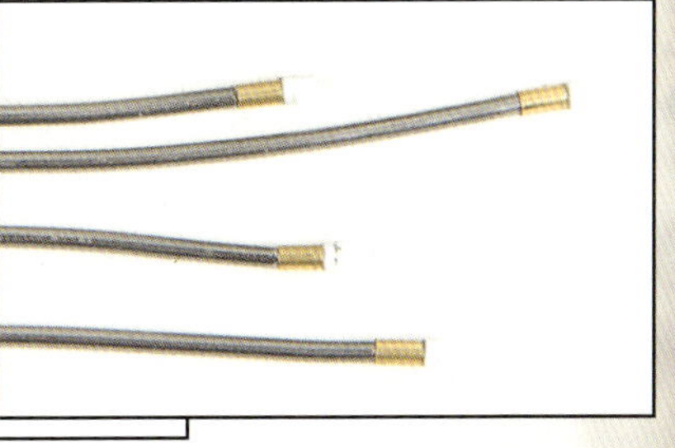

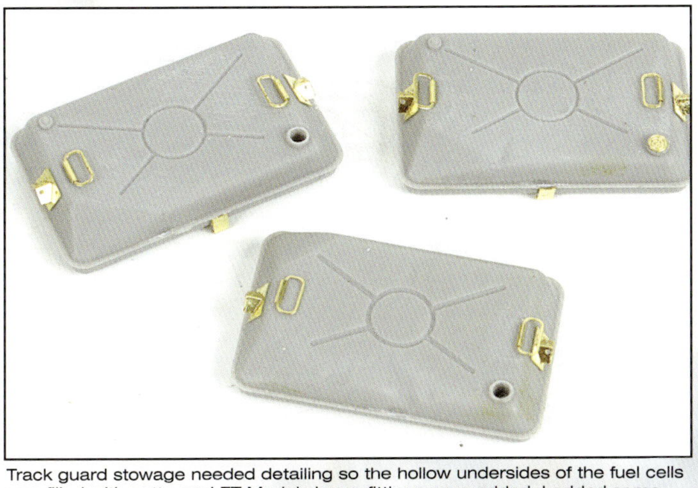

Track guard stowage needed detailing so the hollow undersides of the fuel cells was filled with putty, and ET Models brass fittings were added. I added some dents to the edges of the cells and drilled out the filler caps on two of them.

I assembled the ET Models track guards and then used a mini drill with a burr to create the irregular edge where they were torch cut from the hull.

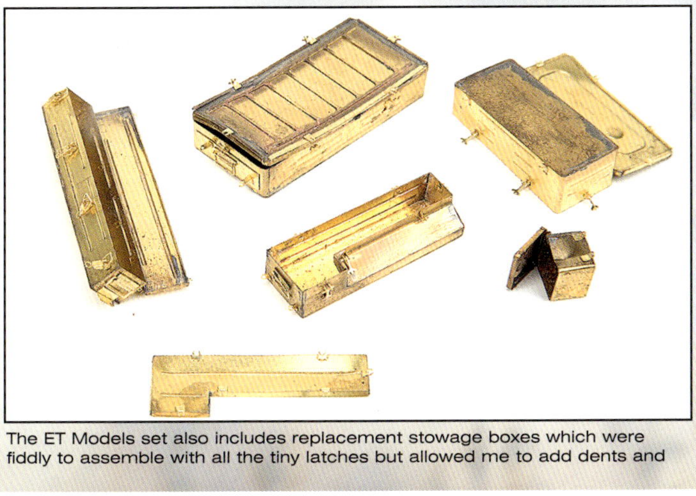

The ET Models set also includes replacement stowage boxes which were fiddly to assemble with all the tiny latches but allowed me to add dents and to create damage that would have been difficult to do with the plastic kit parts.

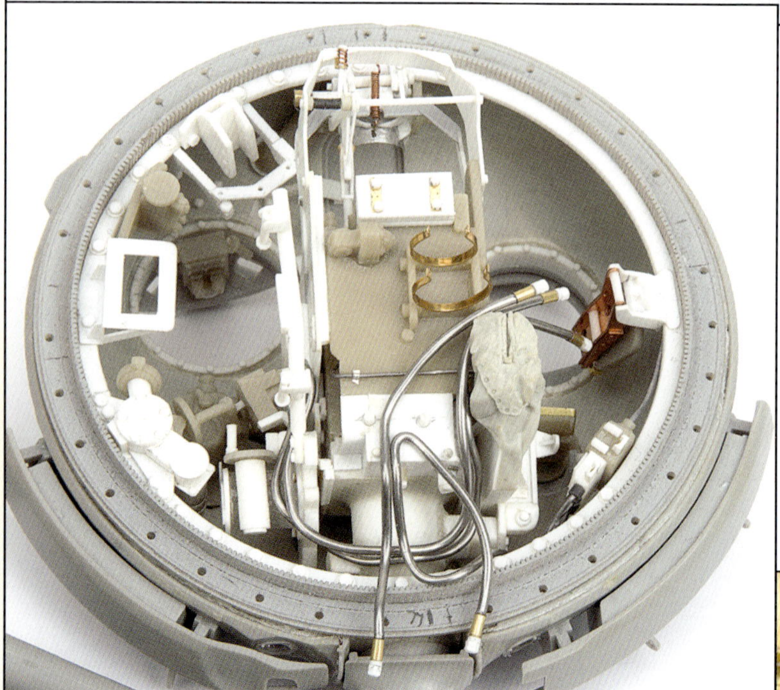

Finally I was able to bring together all the components in a dry fit to see just how well it recreated the look of the real scene. At this stage the additional fine debris is missing but the main components are here and everything looks suitably chaotic.

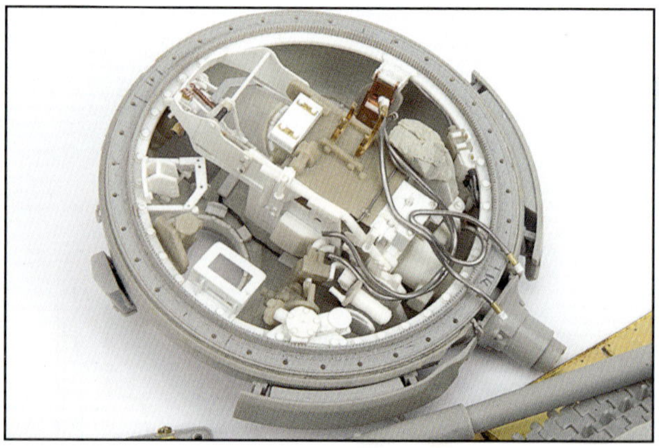

The complex upturned turret was one of the most challenging parts of the construction and the hydraulic hoses draped across the top of the turret really add to the dilapidated look of the turret.

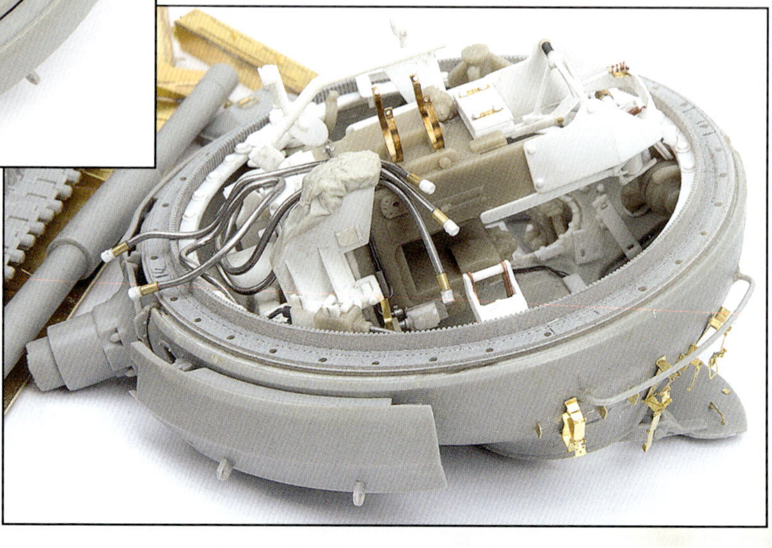

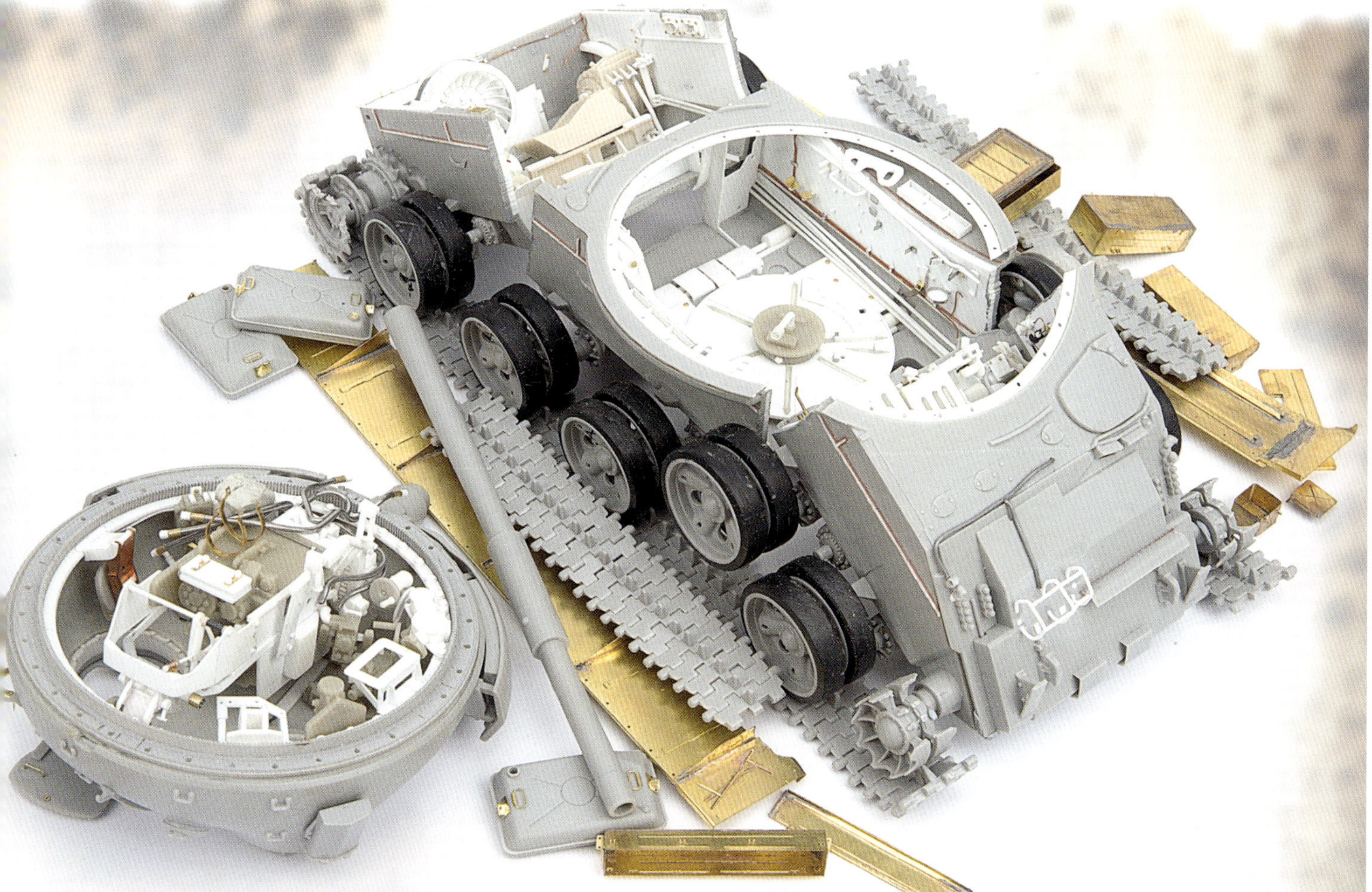

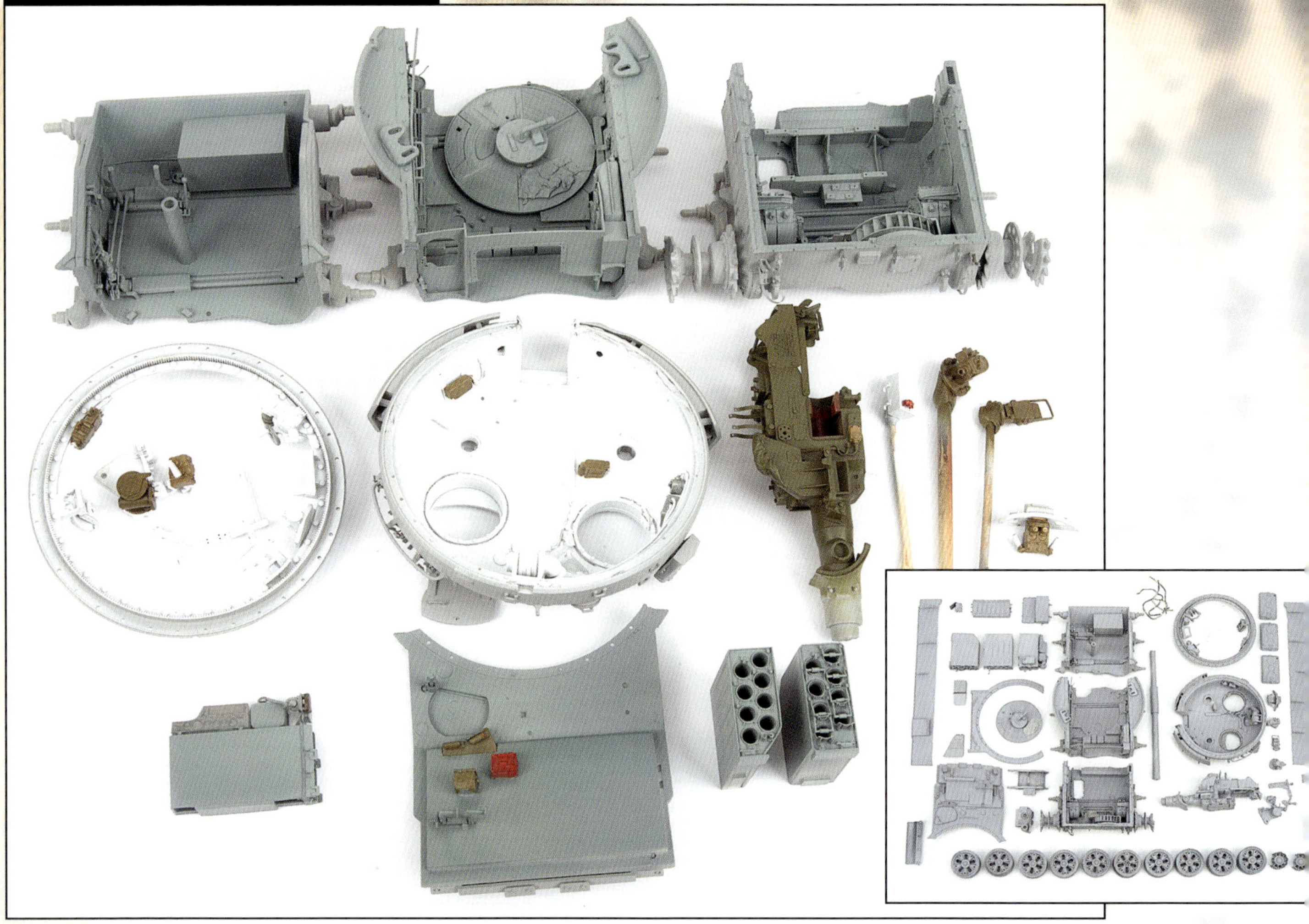

Painting gets underway and begins with spraying all the parts with Mr Primer Surfacer before moving onto the colours for the interior. My plan was to work on the interior first and then to mask it an paint the exterior. Working from the colour photos I mixed a blue grey for the insides of the lower hull, the turret interior was painted in white and the gun in the Russian olive green which was also custom mixed to match the photos.

With the base colours on the breech I added the faded red colours around the mouth of the breech using several tones of red.

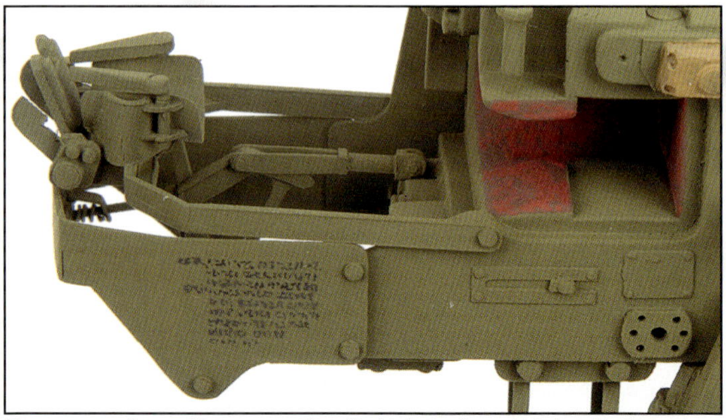

The gun recoil guard has some stencilled information which I replicated using dark grey oil paint to create the illusion of lettering by painting assorted squiggles and shapes. At normal viewing distances this looks just like actual lettering.

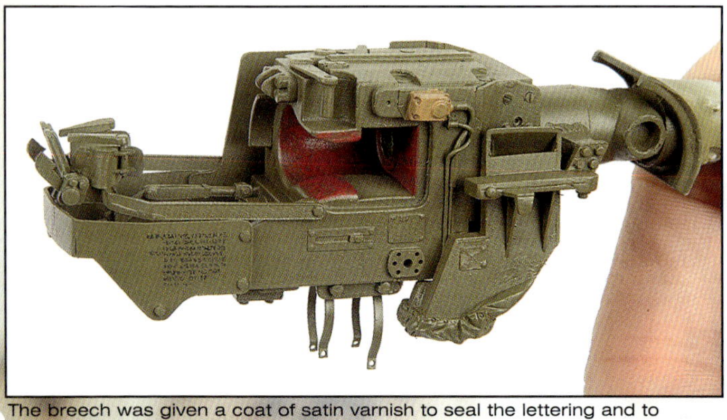

The breech was given a coat of satin varnish to seal the lettering and to prepare for the weathering stage.

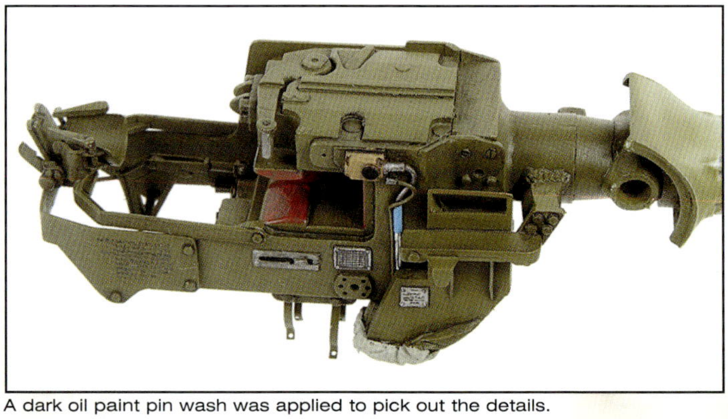

A dark oil paint pin wash was applied to pick out the details.

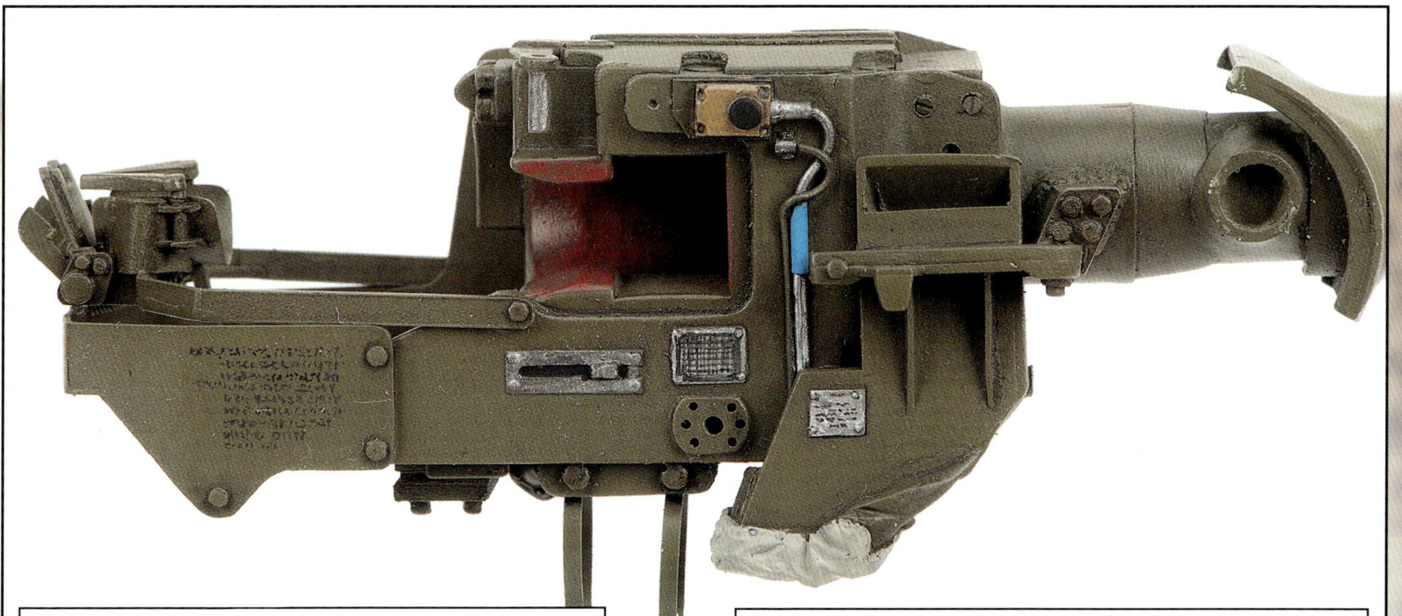

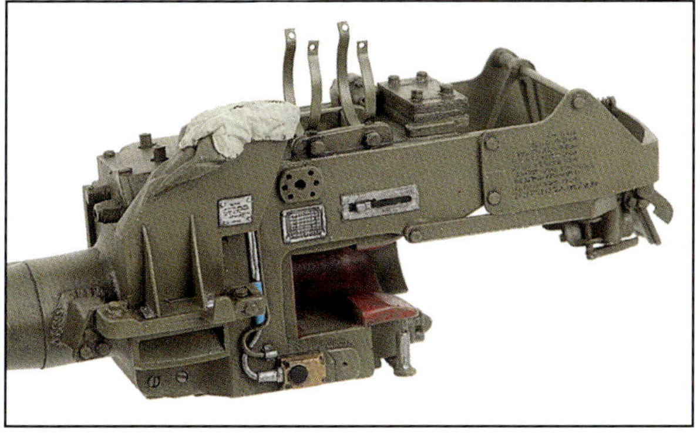

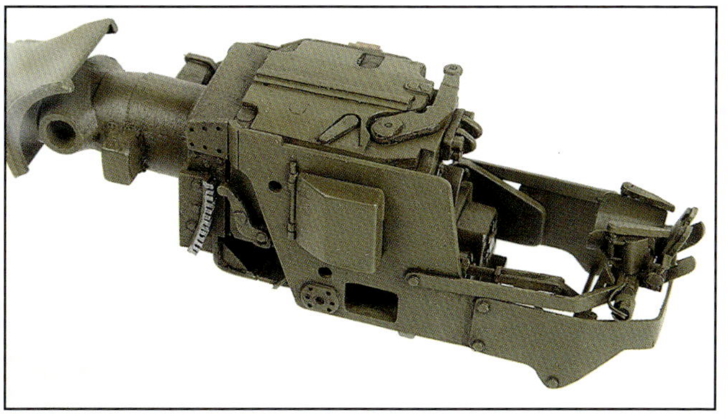

Above Other details like the placards were brush painted and the blue cable sleeve adds a welcome touch of colour. I also started to painted the spent MG ammo sack on the underside of the gun.

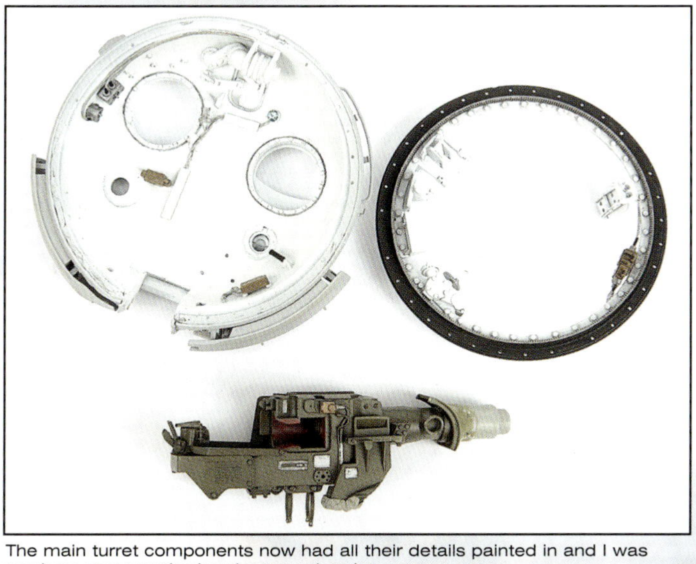

The main turret components now had all their details painted in and I was ready to start weathering the turret interior.

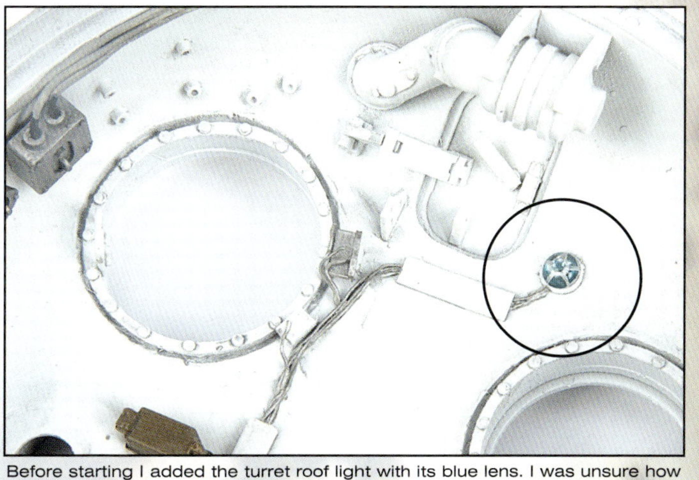

Before starting I added the turret roof light with its blue lens. I was unsure how best to make this but opted to use a headlamp lens which was painted with transparent blue. the framing bars were then brush painted over this.

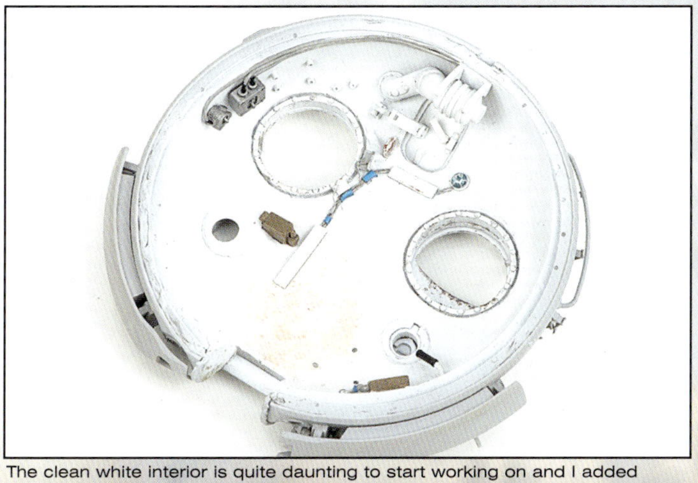

The clean white interior is quite daunting to start working on and I added some subtle washes with rusty tones for where rainwater had collected inside the turret.

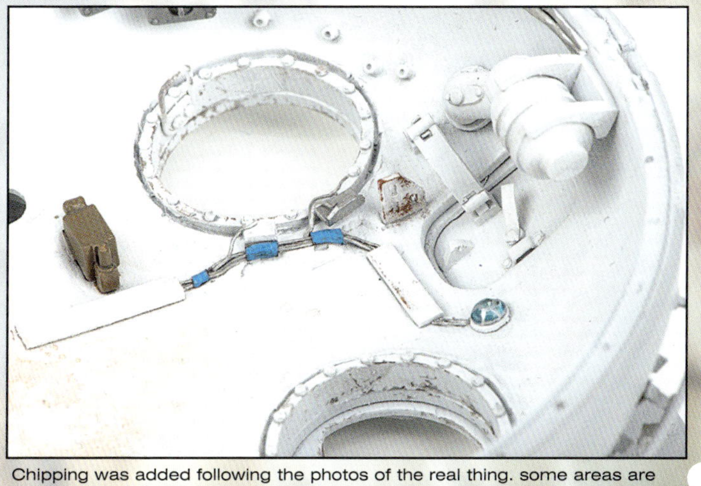

Chipping was added following the photos of the real thing. some areas are badly damaged whilst others appear factory fresh.

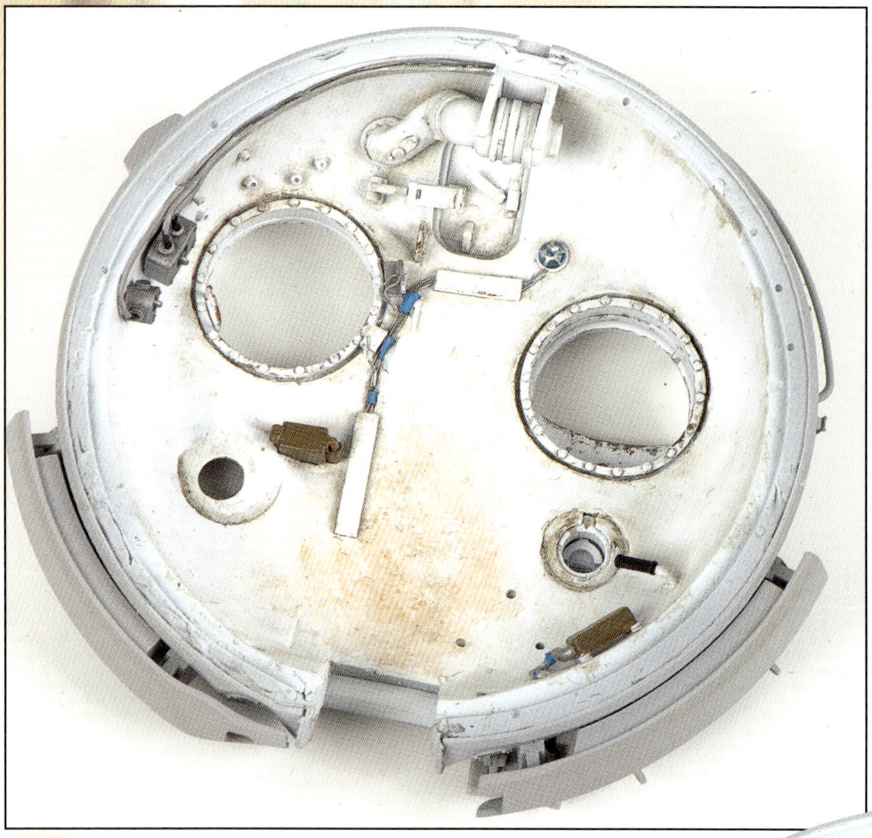

Above Adding more thin oil washes to the turret builds up the intensity of the collected dirt and with the turret upside down I needed to bear in mind just where and how the dirt inside would collect.

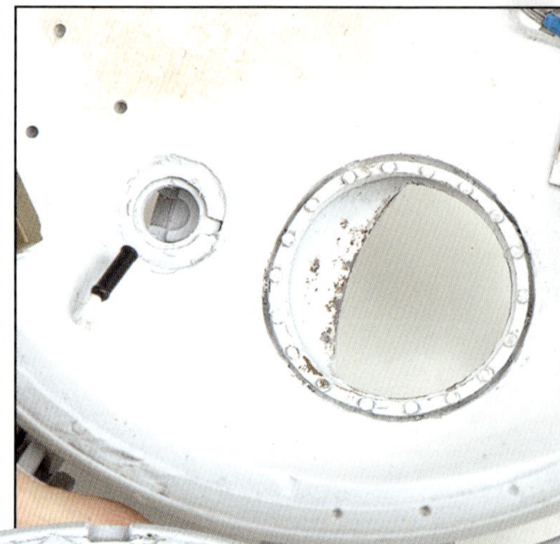

Above Rust stains from the mounting points on the turret wall were added with oil colours which are ideal for these blended effects

Above The big rusty puddle in the centre of the roof looks good here and with hindsight I wish I had left this as it appears here but the photos of the real turret show a collection of rusty particles that have been deposited here when the turret was dumped upside down.

Left Rainmarks down the other side of the turret were added with oil paints taking care to ensure that they correspond to the turret's eventual resting position which is a nose down alignment.

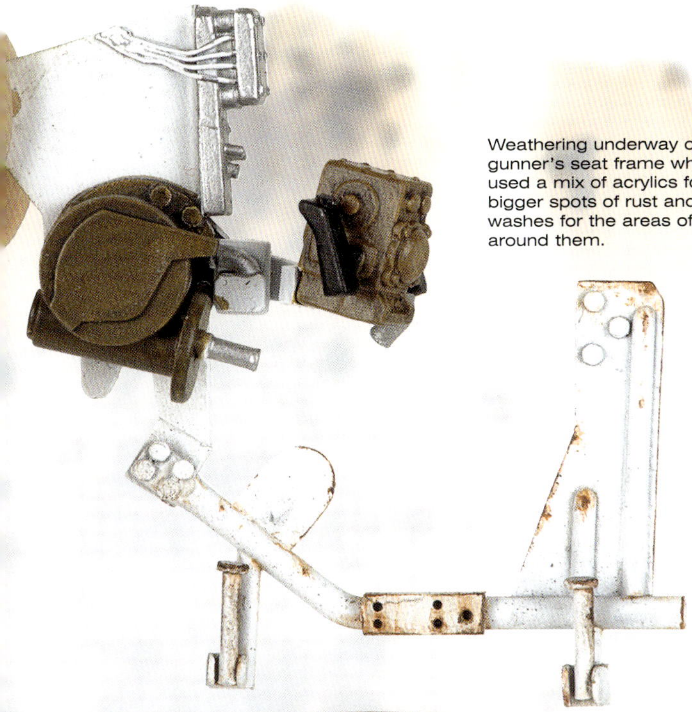

Weathering underway on the gunner's seat frame where is used a mix of acrylics for the bigger spots of rust and oil washes for the areas of staining around them.

To create the rusty particles I mixed together some different rust toned pigments. I painted a puddle of pigment fixer in the turret and scattered on the mix. I was not entirely happy with how this looked and I felt it did not really get the look that I wanted and it looked very stark against the white base.

The turret ring was also weathered with selected rusty areas which were again modelled on the photos of the real thing. I was still not at all happy with the look of the pigments so I had to consider how to improve the look of this area. The pigment fixer had done an excellent job of sticking them to the turret so t=it was not possible to just brush them away.

Above I used a curved scalpel blade to scrape away the majority of the pigments taking care not to damage the underlying paint or to create any unnatural-looking edges or harsh transitions. This process too some time but the result was much closer to the look that I had be trying to create.

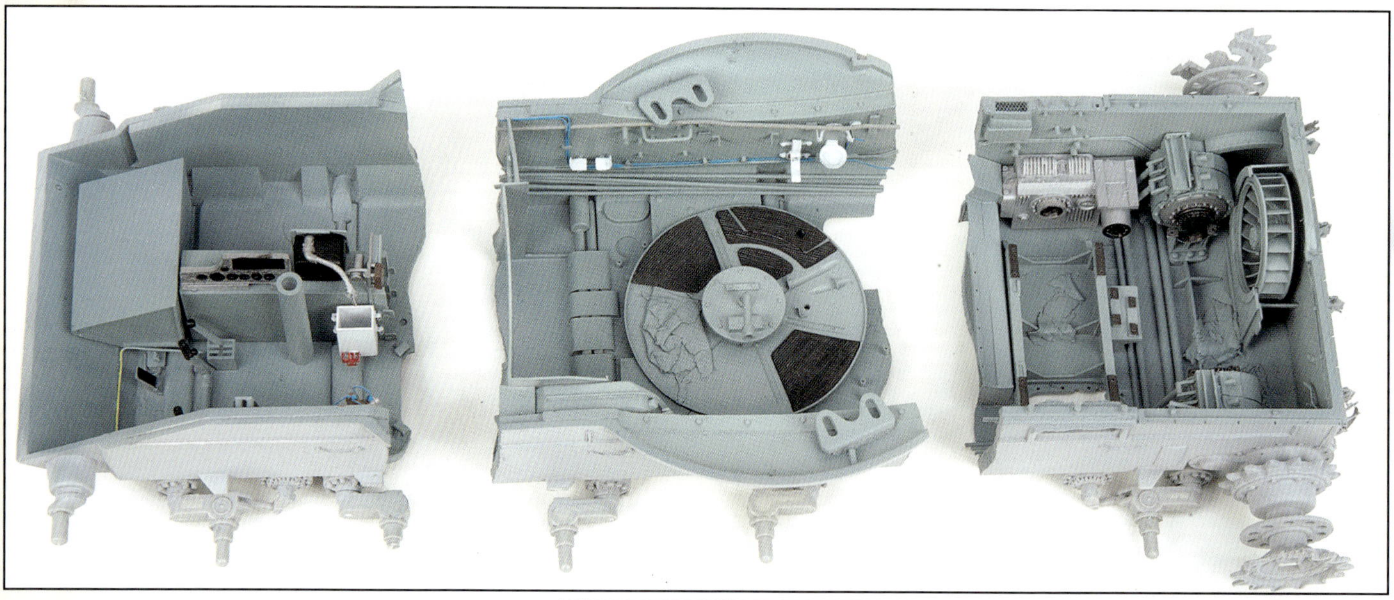

At this point I moved onto the hull where all the small detailed colour elements were picked out in preparation for the whole thing getting extremely dirty. The metallic parts in the engine bay were painted using the new Vallejo metallic acrylic colours.

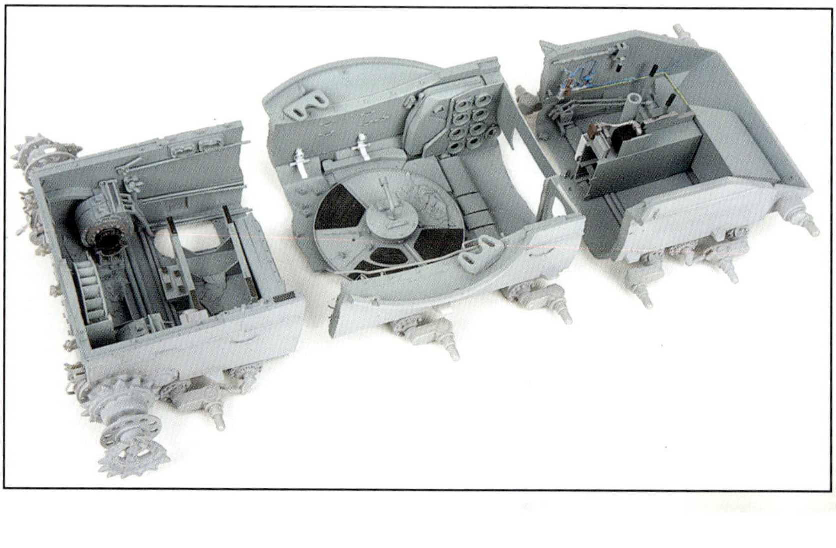

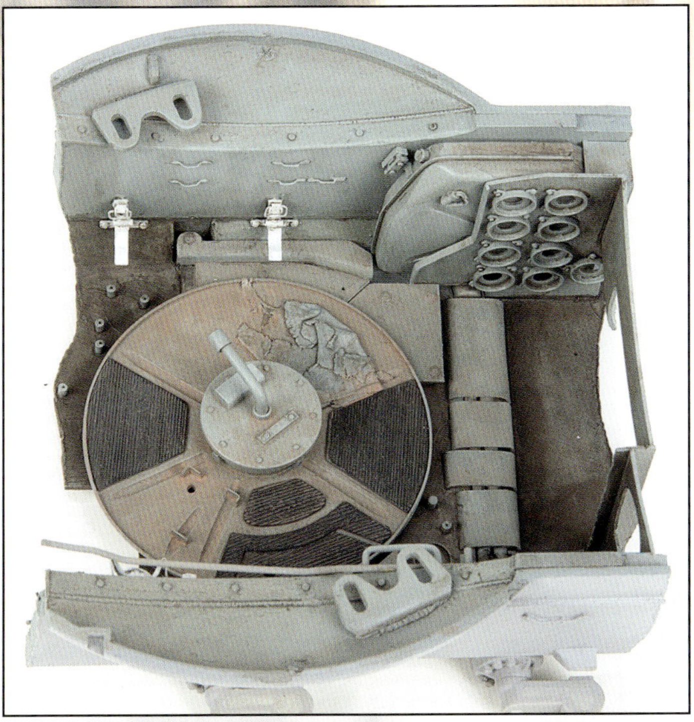

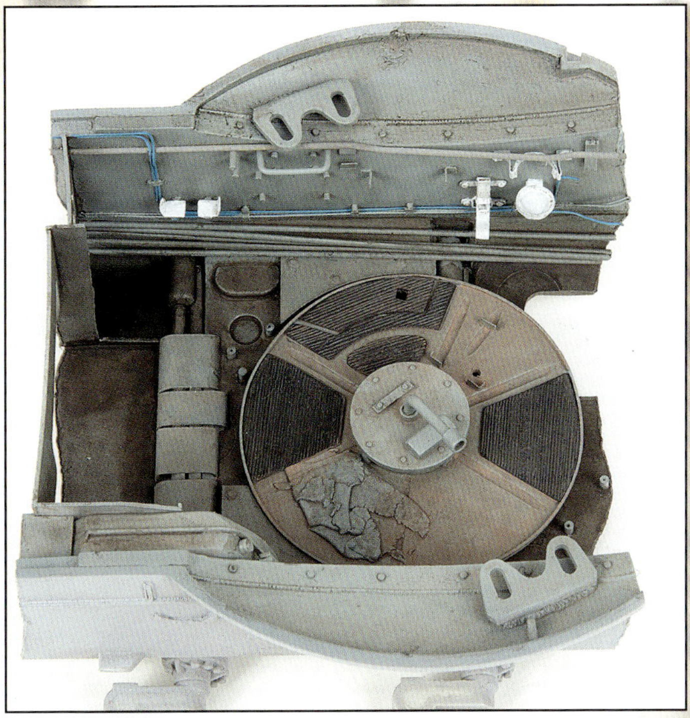

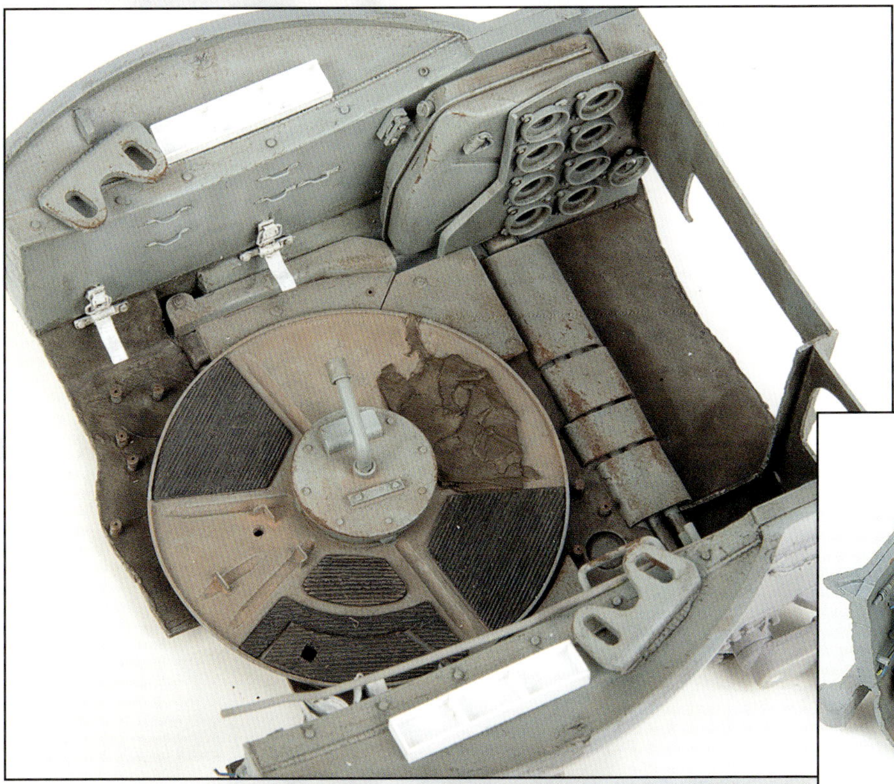

Starting to get dirty and the centre hull section was weathered with numerous washes built up in multiple layers. The floor was almost completely obscured with an opaque dark black - brown acrylic wash to replicate all the collected oil and debris seen in the photos. I was pleased that these washes also adjusted the tone of the underlying grey colour, adjusting it match that seen on the real vehicle. The turret basket in the photos has a very different pale brown appearance and again I used a wash of Lifecolor acrylics to add this tone with more dilute washes of the same tone also applied to some of the surrounding raised floor panels.

Left Area of rust chipping were added to the floor panels and to other selected areas of the interior as shown in the photos. As well as a fine brush a piece of sponge was also used to apply these rust chips. The discarded oil-soaked fabric lying on the turret basket floor was also defined using a mix of dark brown tones to do this.

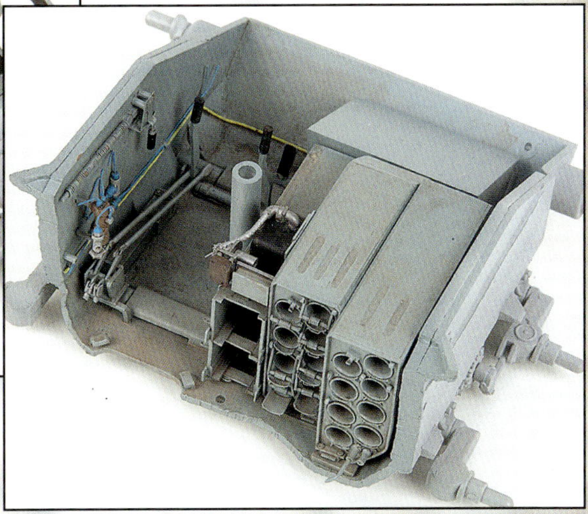

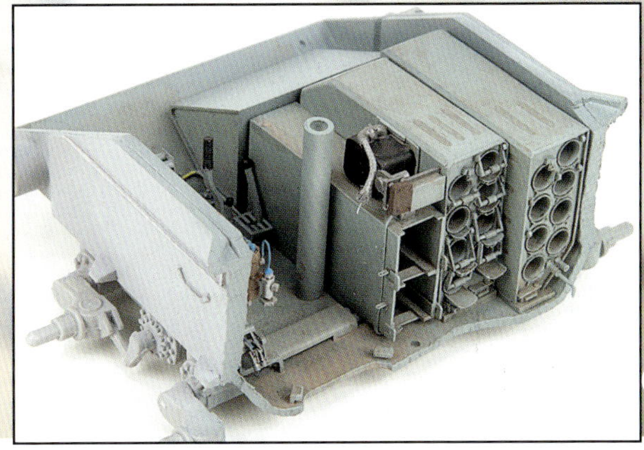

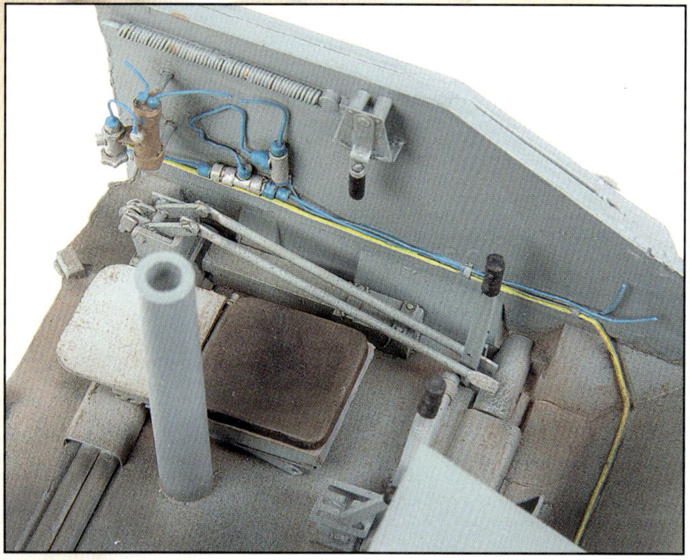

The brightly coloured pipework adds a welcome splash of colour to the grey interior. Dust and dirt washes have been applied to the lower hull areas.

The battery rack has the instrument panel painted and I used a yellowed white to paint the dials for an aged appearance.

Dry fitting the battery rack into the hull to check that the finish matches the rest of the interior. When working with lots of separate parts like this it is vital to keep checking.

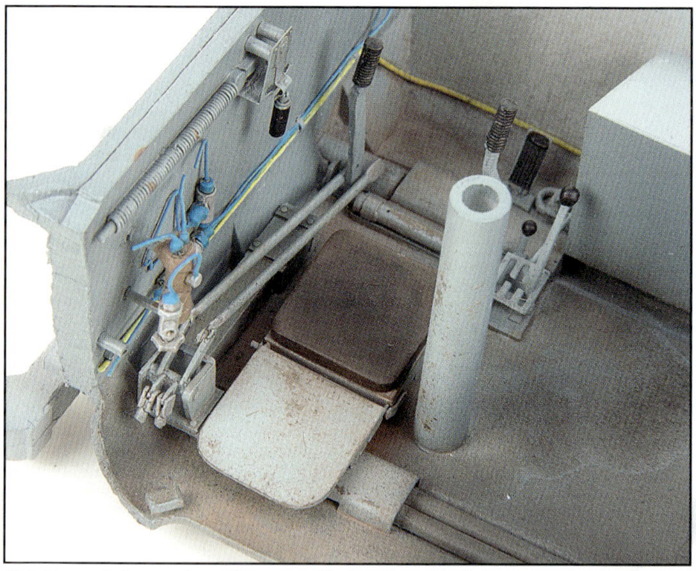

Subtle scratches and scuffs are applied to the folded down seat back.

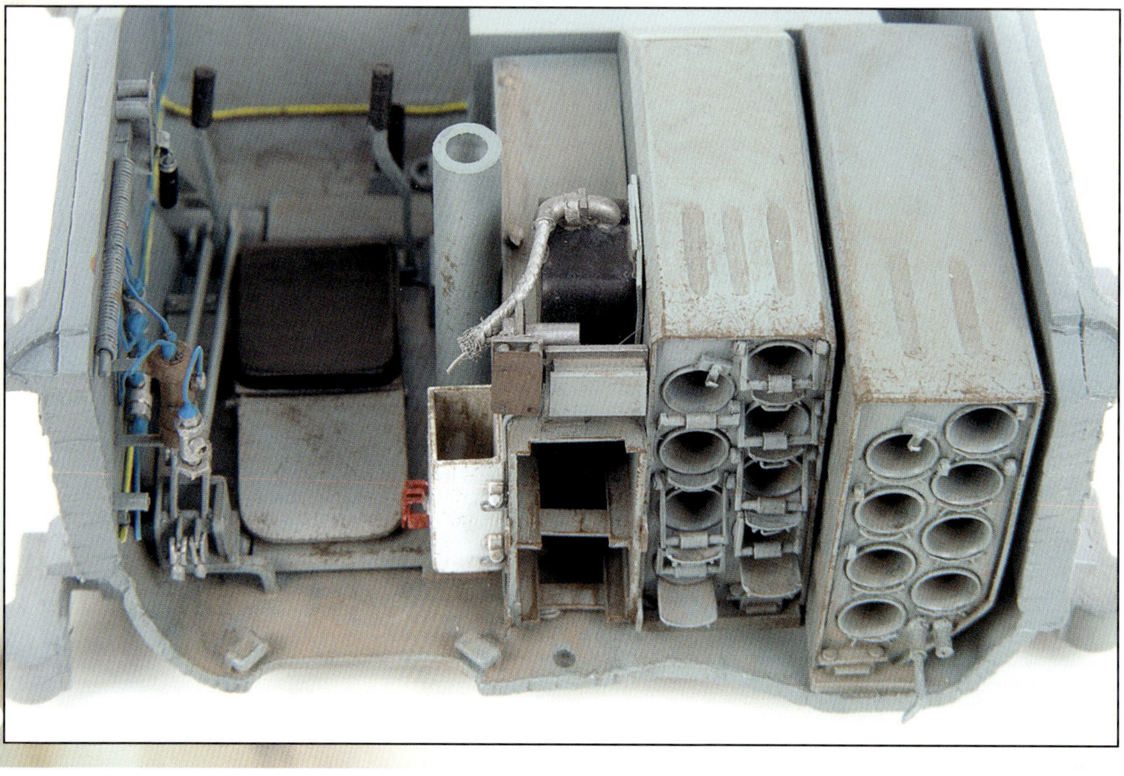

Similarly chips and scratches were added to the edges of the ammo bins using sponge and a fine brush to add these.

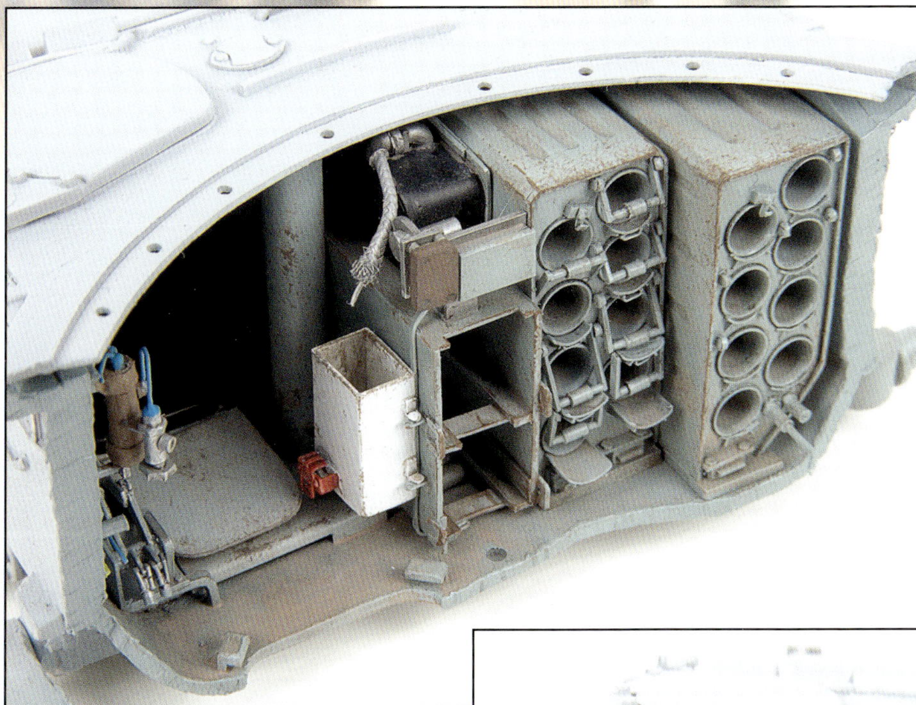

The photos of the real vehicle were a real help in getting the correct look of the wear and damage in these areas. I was approaching the time where the hull roof would be fixed on permanently so there would no longer be any opportunity to access the interior. The battery rack and ammo bins would not be glued in place yet as they can slide into the hull even when the roof is fitted.

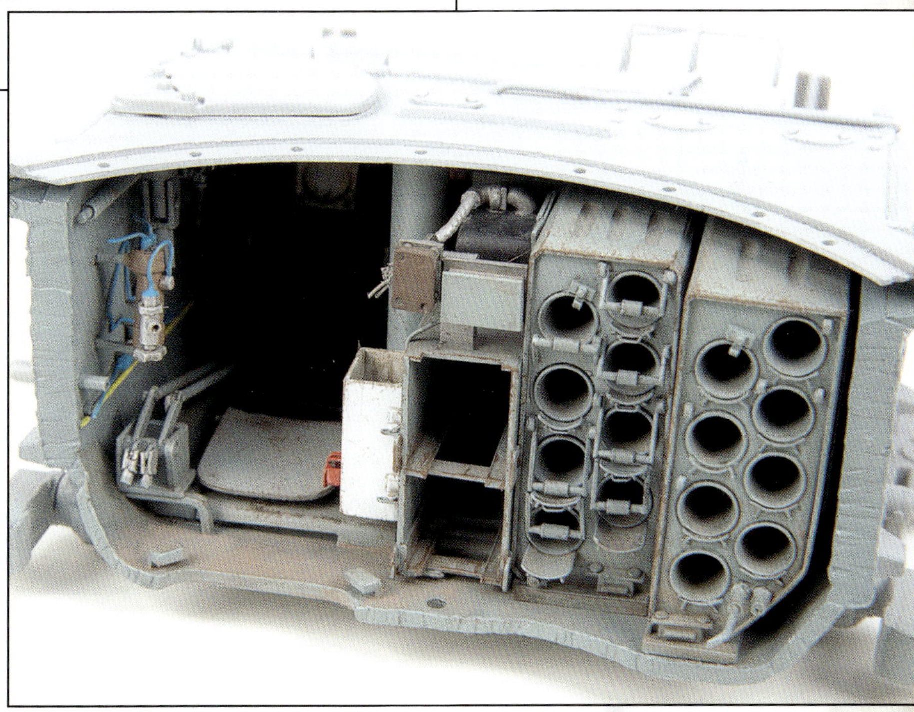

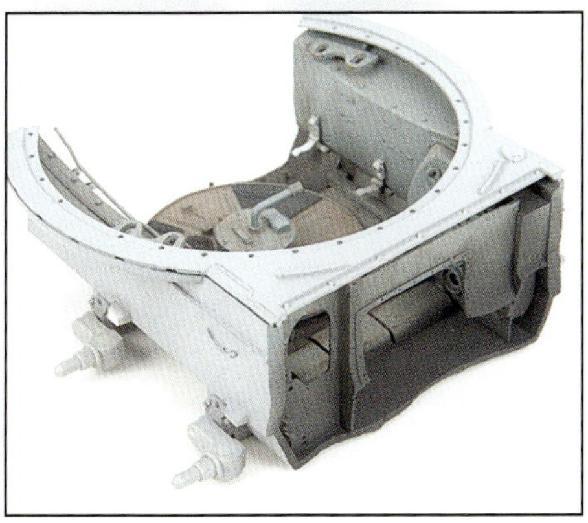

The engine bay was airbrushed with a suitable grimy black oil shade to reflect the finish of these parts on the real thing. This was also applied to the firewall on the centre tub section and carried through onto the floor of the centre tub.

The bow roof is glued on and the joint seam lines are filled and sanded to hide and sign of the joint. I also had to add the remains of the track guard which runs across the joint line. In the same way the roof was also added to the centre hull tub.

The hull was masked using pieces of foam supplemented with masking tape to protect the interior. After the primer a base of a rust brown was applied with the intention of applying a hairspray chipping technique.

Top coats of green were applied using different tones and leaving some of the underlying brown showing through in places.

Scrubbing off the top layers to expose the underlying paint produced this effect which I was not completely happy with.

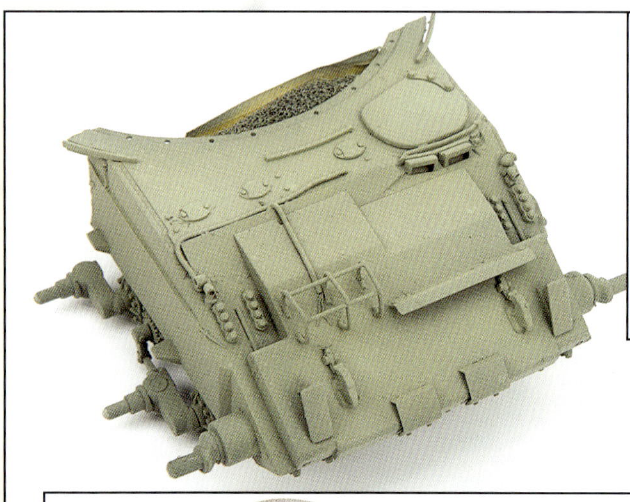

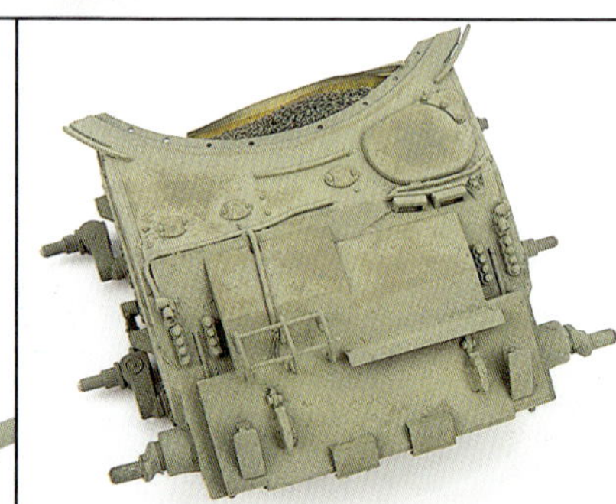

I decided that I would also adjust the colour of the green by mixing more yellow and making it more faded so everything went back into the paint booth. Rather than use the hairspray technique again I decided to brush paint the chips and worn paint effects. I began by adding some darker tones to represent older layers of paint exposed beneath the faded top coat. This was followed by drybrushing brown tones in areas where the paint had been worn away.

I used a big flat brush to scrub the areas of corrosion with almost a drybrush technique, building up the different tones.

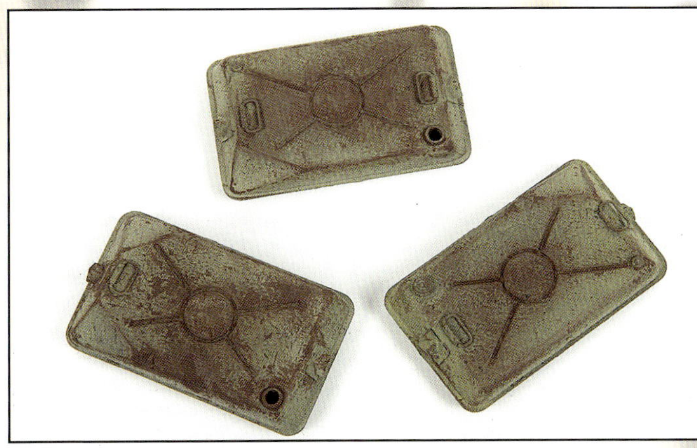

The same technique was used on the fuel cells but also using a fine brush to apply chips and scratches as well as the drybrushing.

The track guards seen here at the end of this process with oil washes to be applied over this next.

Above The turret which will be upside down still had to be weathered to reflect the years spent outside before it was flipped off the hull. I added areas of darker paint as well as many rain marks and streaks.

Returning to the hull a fine brush was used to add the various chips and rust spots across all three sections.

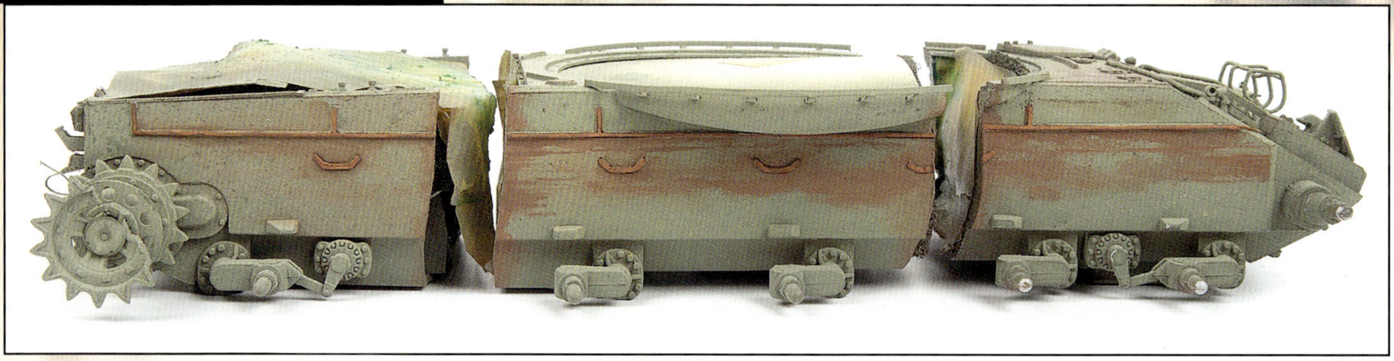

Areas of rust were loosely brushed along the length of the lower hull to match the real vehicle and as most of this would be covered in dried mud there was no need to be too precise.

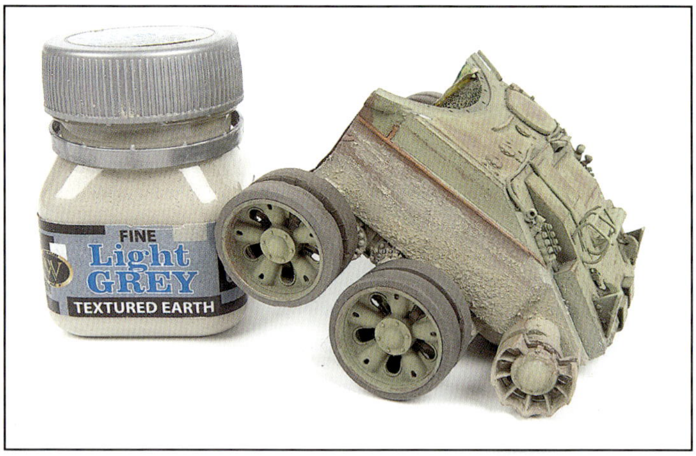

I used a brush to apply Wilder textured earth over the lower hull and suspension mounts, leaving clean areas where the rusted parts would show through.

A quick blast with the airbrush unified the appearance of the muddy finish and I then started to work over the rusty areas with different oil washes. The oil washes were also used to add stains to the rusted parts of the drive sprockets.

Acrylic paint rust chips and spots were added to the turret and then oil paint was used to apply rust stains on top of this. Nothing does rust stain better than oil paint and it is endlessly adjustable allowing you to get just the required look, most of this sadly disappears when the turret is inverted.

The hull rear which we have not really looked at before but you can see how the paint effects have been carried over this too and rust stains have been added.

Strangely it proved more demanding working on a three part hull rather than the more normal single piece to keep a unified approach across the parts so that they look cohesive when they are brought together. I started working over the more heavily worn areas with oil paint washes in rust tones which also discoloured the green paint in places too. This slightly contradictory process of applying rust oil tones over rust acrylics seems to adjust the look of these areas to impart a more natural aged look to the rusted parts.

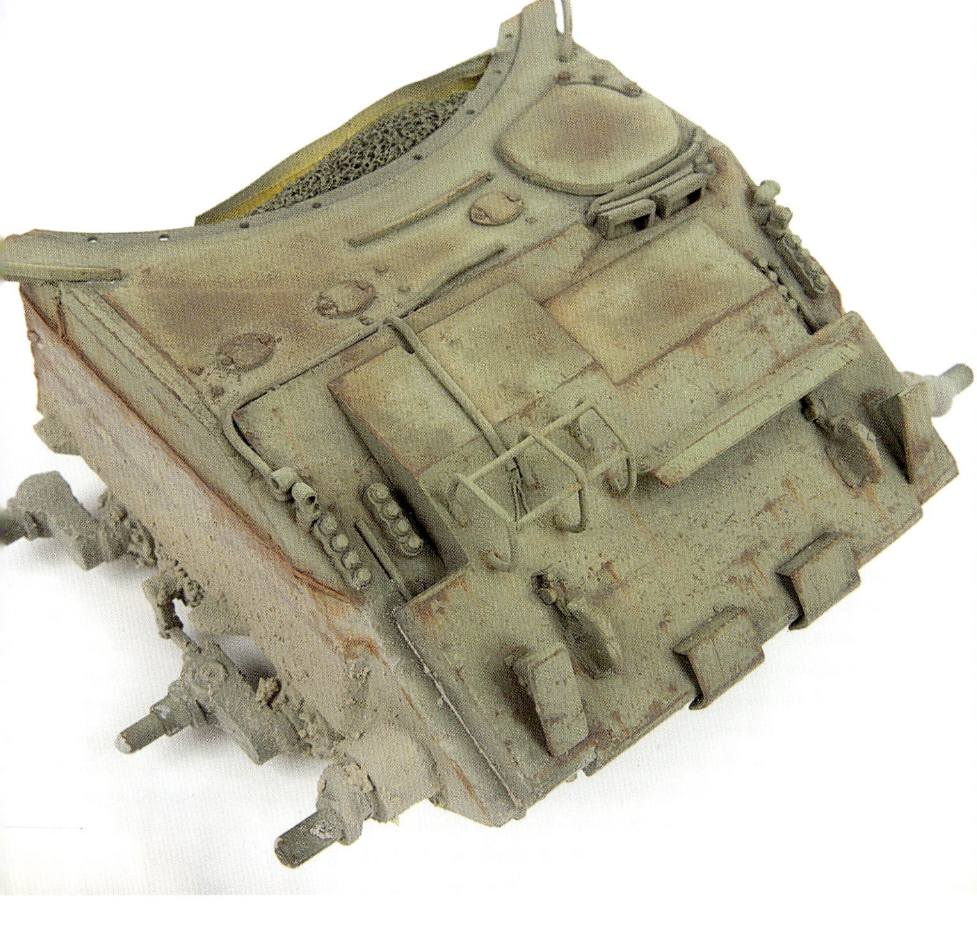

I brushed rust coloured pigments along the torch-cut edges where the heat has stripped away the paint.

The roadwheels were finished individually before being installed onto the hull. I was careful to match the colour of the old rubber tyres to the real vehicle and the areas of corrosion on the hubs. Leaking seals mean that many of the wheels are heavily stained so this was also replicated. With the wheels fitted I thought it was probably safe to remove the internal masking, always an exciting moment!

Below the next stage was to look at the torch-cut edges of the hull sections which have a mix of colours with touches of rust. A mix of dry brushing and washes were used on the edges before touches of rust were added.

The pictures of the real turret show a collection of small parts and debris that have dropped into the upturned turret roof. Creating this mix of small metal parts, fastenings and plates is never simple nor is achieving a realistic randomness to their position. Although the huge gun will lie over these I felt it was important to replicate these details. I scoured assorted old photoetched frets for suitable pieces that could be adapted as well as making some plates from pewter sheet. Photoetched bolts and washers were also utilised along with pewter strip straps. These parts were painted and then glued into position inside the turret.

With this done the gun could at last be fitted into the turret. The gun mount is a tight push fit into the front of the turret so I was able to adjust the angle of the gun and to fit the gun control / Gunner's seat frame assembly alongside it before gluing the gunmount to lock the gun position. With this done the turret ring with the rest of the turret fixtures could be added and glued into place. The base of the gun was treated with wet oil effects using Wilder Old Grease paint to get this very realistic finish matching the photos of the real gun.

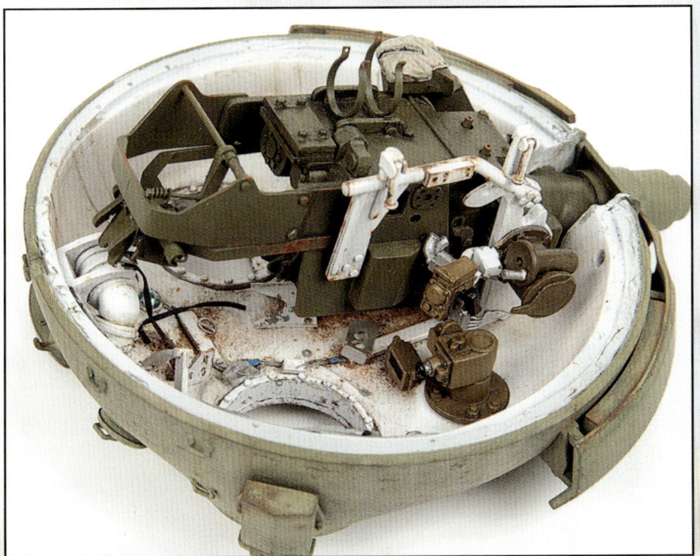

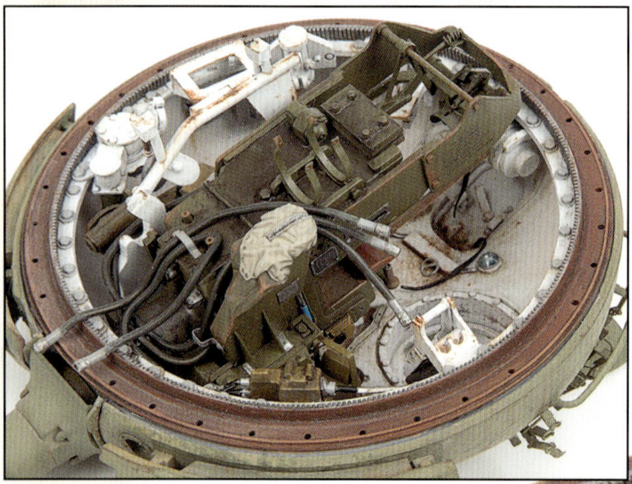

The final job was to install the hydraulic hoses and I had to consult my build images to remind myself of how they all fitted into the turret. They were glued into place working from the lowest points. Once they were attached I made a pair of pewter foil clamps which hold the hoses in position and these were added on to the base of the gun and the from of the MG mount.

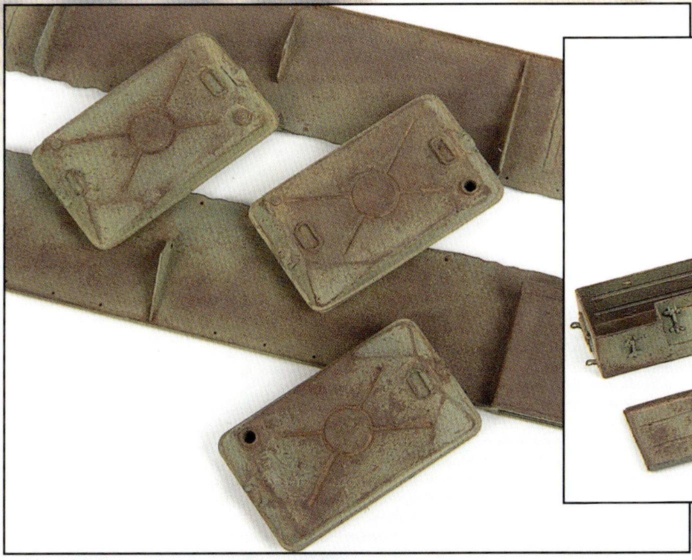

More work on the larger separates with oil washes of rust tones used to age the finish of these parts.

Returning to the inside of the hull and I wanted to recreate the dirty oily residue in the bottom of the engine bay. Once again I used Wilder Old Grease for this but I mixed into this some dark grey pigments to give a textures finish to these areas.

In the bottom of the centre hull section I wanted to create the accumulated dirt and debris that I could see in the photos. I used a mix of different pigment colours to create this. They were placed into position using a paintbrush and I applied some pigment fixer to secure them.

Once the fixer had dried the floor areas looked like this.

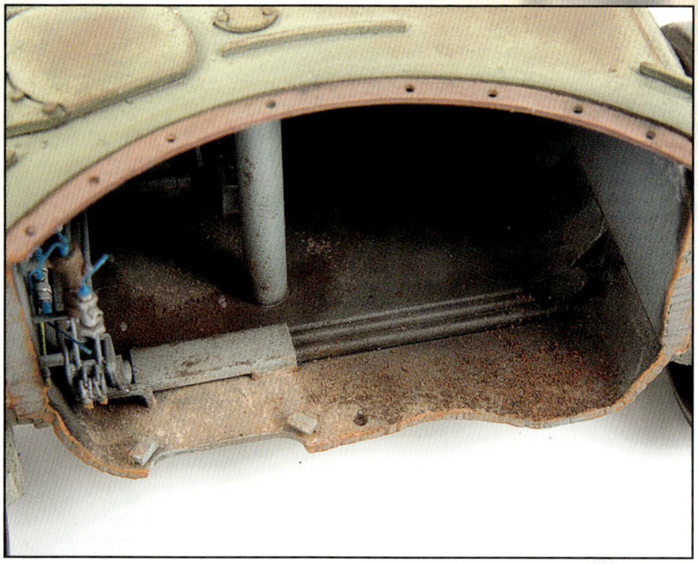

I treated the front hull section floor in the same way but using different coloured pigments.

I was now able to glue the turret basket floor into the hull and I began to start adding the pieces of debris that are lying inside the hull. Making these was extremely time-consuming. I used a mix of left over pieces of photoetch from assorted detail sets along with any suitable small kit parts and parts I cut from pewter sheet. These all had to be individually painted and pre-weathered before the were glued into position.

The hull is brought together at this stage after the driver's seat and ammunition bins have now been glued into position.

I started work on a base which was formed from expanded polystyrene with a clay surface which the tracks were set into.

The base was painted to depict areas of wet and dry mud and clumps of static grass from the Joefix range were added.

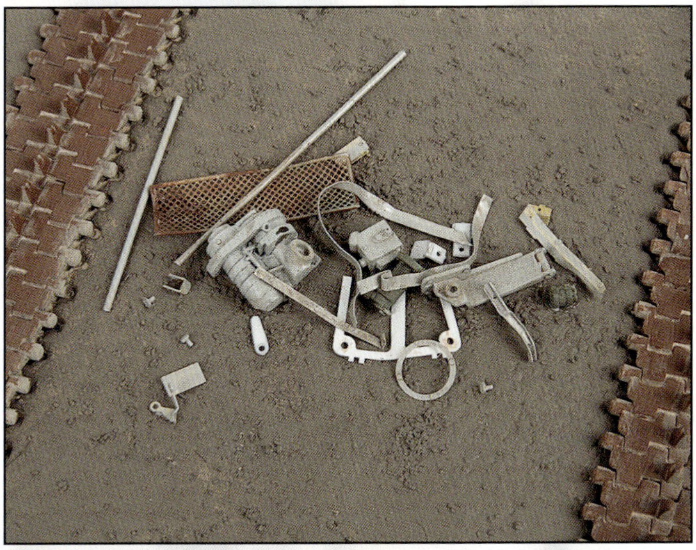

Before adding the vehicle I had to add more assorted debris that had dropped through the gaps in the hull. This was once again a mix of suitable looking kit parts, spare photoetch and even plain plastic rod. Positioning the parts takes some experimentation in order to get a natural random look to the group with a mix of large and some very small parts.

Another feature that had to be added was the pooled molten metal from where the hull had been torch cut. To replicate this I used Mr Surfacer which I brushed onto the base following the cut lines on the hull. I went over these several time to build up the depth.

The puddles of molten metal were painted in a dull silver colour and I also added areas of spilt oil and fuel with these concentrated around the engine bay. I also blended the mud and debris up around the tracks where the vehicle has been stationary for so long that it has settled into the ground.

Small pieces of debris were glued into the floor and the rusty areas were added to the right hand ammunition bin where the cutting torch has cut away trays and other fixtures from the front face.

I used black pigments to apply selected scorch marks on and around the torch cut areas.

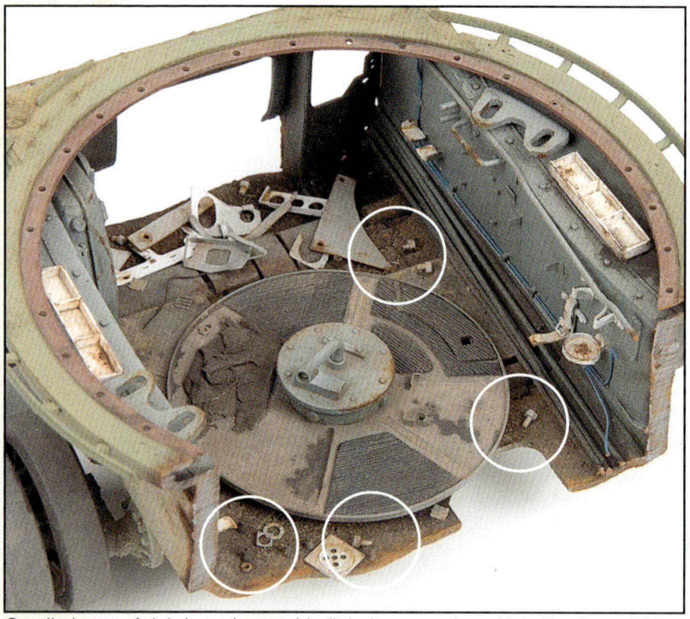

Small pieces of debris and scratchbuilt bolts were placed into the floor of the centre section

On the back of the firewall I used rust coloured pigments to soften the torch cut areas and blending them up the firewall as seen in the photos.

In the engine bay similar small pieces were added to the floor along with some bits of cable. As with all these parts they were individually painted before being placed.

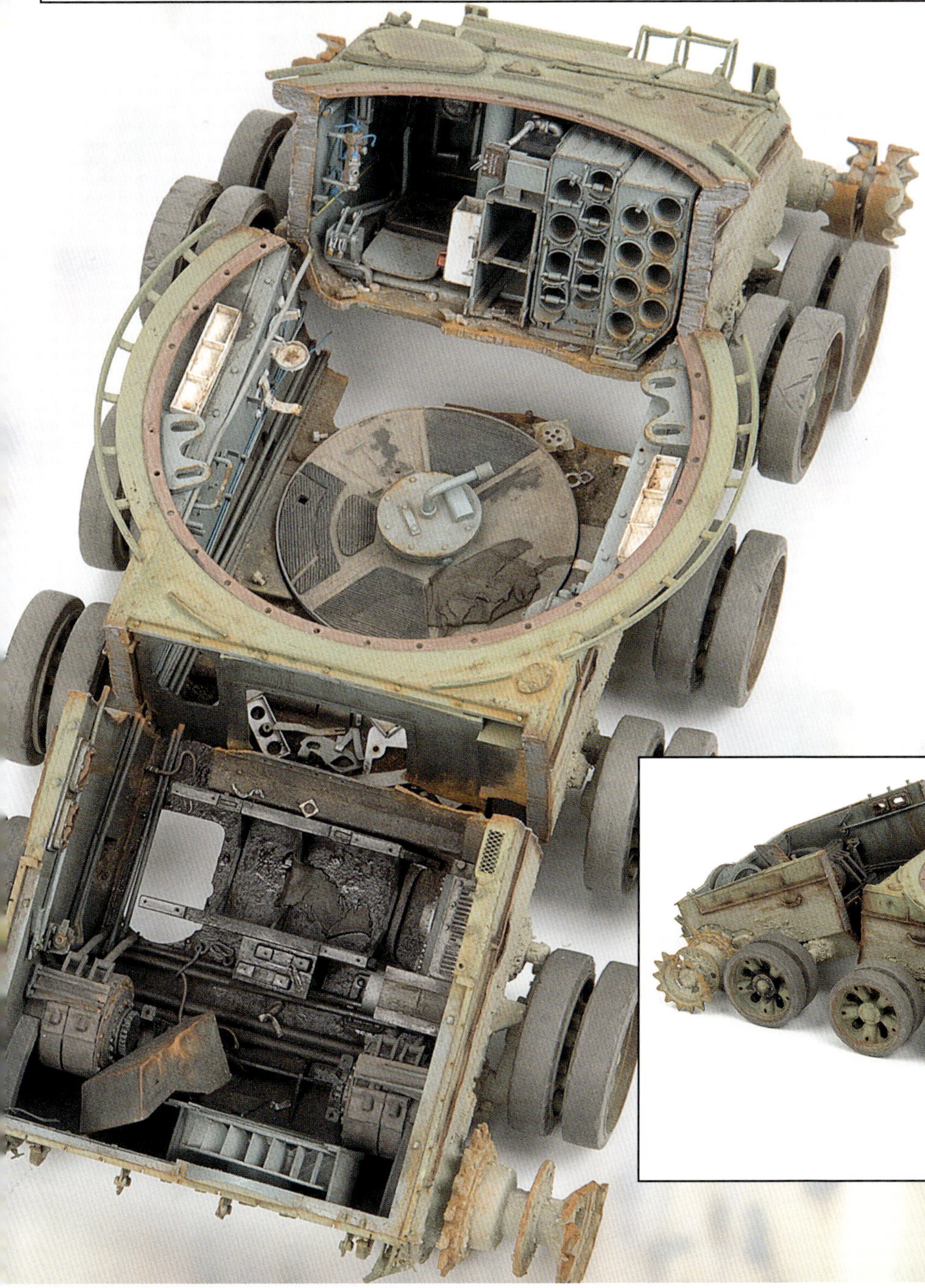

At last I felt happy to move on to bringing together all of the parts on the base which would inevitably restrict access so it was important to be certain that the hull pieces were ready before moving ahead. Bringing the parts together is important to check the consistency of the finish and to make sure that it looks like one vehicle that has been cut up.

The engine section was fixed into position first, locking the sprocket teeth into the track I used PVA glue on the contact areas of the roadwheel to fix the piece in place.

The bow section was fitted next followed by the centre section. I started to add the clumps of grass and weeds that had started to sprout up around the hull.

I pre-painted both the clumps of static grass and some dried plants that would be used for the weeds with my own mix of Lifecolor acrylics.

I used tweezers to pinch out the top sections of the plant which made a convincing weed to glue into place on the base. The pictures show weeds growing up through the tracks in some places so I replicated this.

The process of building up the groundwork is underway here with the hull starting to look like it id embedded into the ground.

The turret was then glued in position and then I began to position the track guards and the other assorted debris. I had to cut the track guards in to two sections in order to achieve an arrangement similar to those of the real vehicle. Once again each piece was test fitted in position in order to achieve a realistic haphazard pile of parts. It is all too easy to make them look artificial when doing this so test fitting is essential. Everything was secured using PVA glue.

Pigments were applied on the tops of the tracks where debris has collected and fixed with pigment fixer. Some pigment was also selectively dusted on to areas of the track guards.

Eventually all the assorted pieces are fixed in place and I began to add some of the tiny parts like bolts, pieces of wire, cables and hoses. These were all collected in preparation for this and pre-painted. I used think lead wire to make up rubber hoses with aluminium tape used to add details like the collars.

Right One of the last items to be added were some items of litter. These were made from some suitably thin paper which was crumpled up and slightly stained before being glued in place.

The crumpled piece of paper lying on the turret floor is another little touch of realism that brings the model to life.

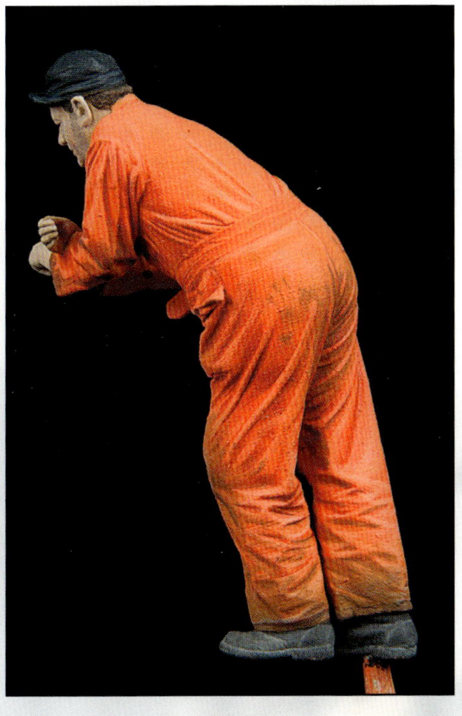

Throughout the progress of the model I had wanted to add some sort of additional interest but I was keen to avoid some of the more usual modelling clichés like the cameraman or cat! The fact that the vehicle had already been cut up and then just left precluded the possibility of having a chap with a cutting torch in the process of cutting it up. Eventually and completely by chance I settled on a mechanic figure from a company called Reedoak. Their figures are based on 3D scans of real people which are then 3D printed in a choice of scales. The casual pose seemed ideal and when the figure arrived it was perfectly suited to lean on the side of the upturned turret. To add a focal point to the model I decided to paint the figure in the high visibility orange overalls that are so common today. I sprayed Lifecolor fluorescent orange which was mixed with a little pale orange over a white primer base. The folds in the clothing is of course completely realistic and the figure was a real pleasure to paint. I had to experiment a little with painting the orange suit and working out how to add shading with out losing the day-glo effect. I then had to add some areas of dirt to the trouser cuffs, elbows, knees and seat. These included some oily fingerprints across the seat where a hand has been wiped.

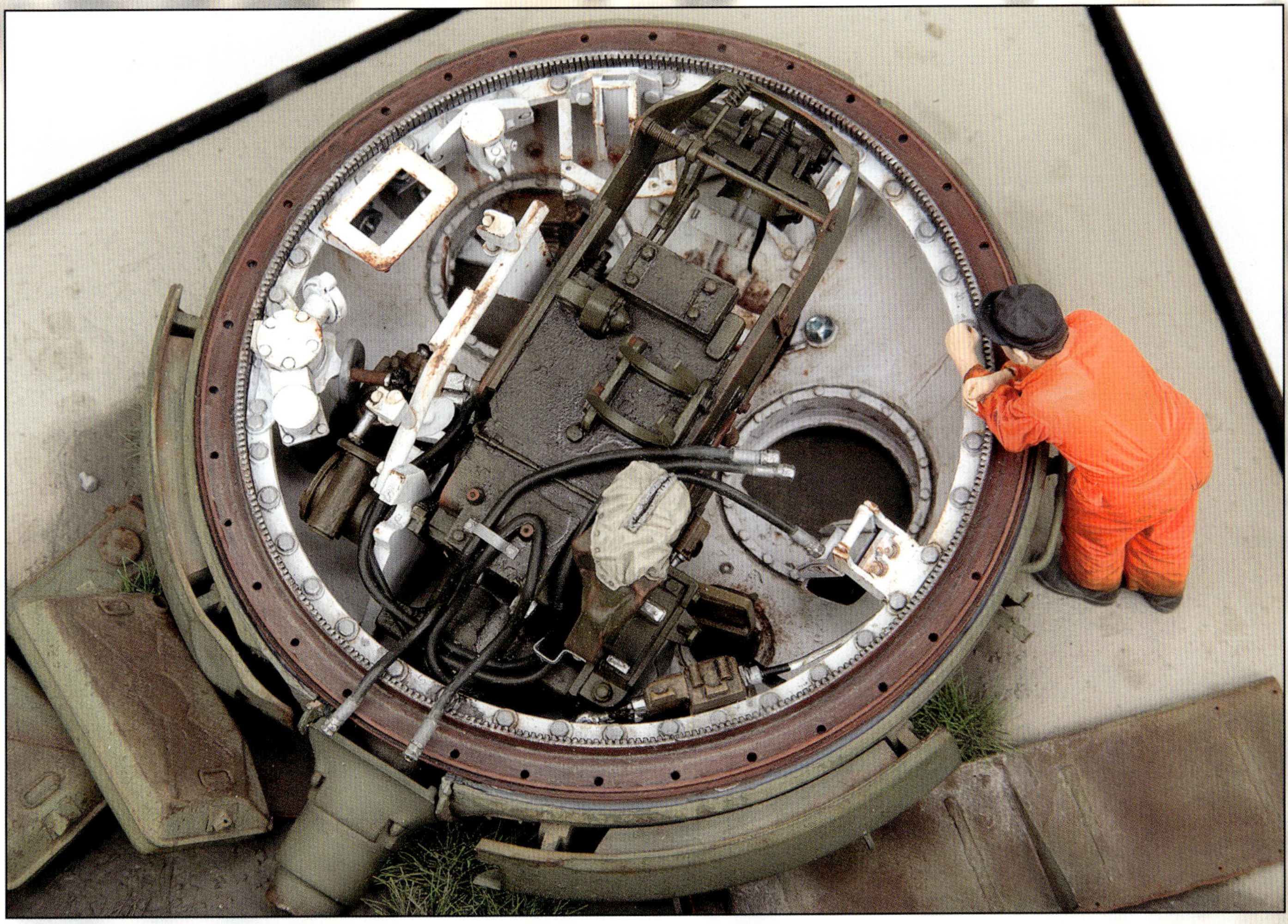

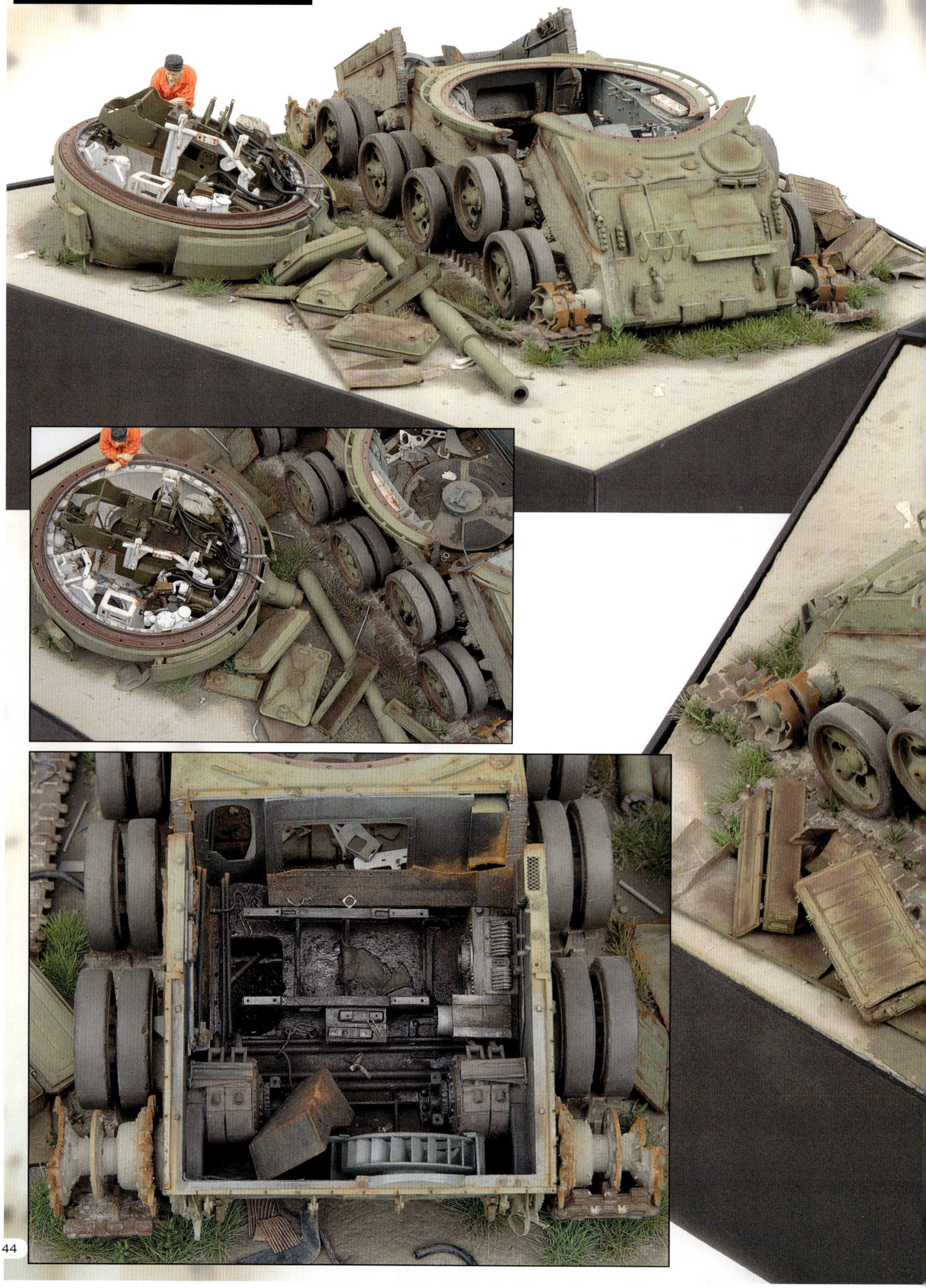

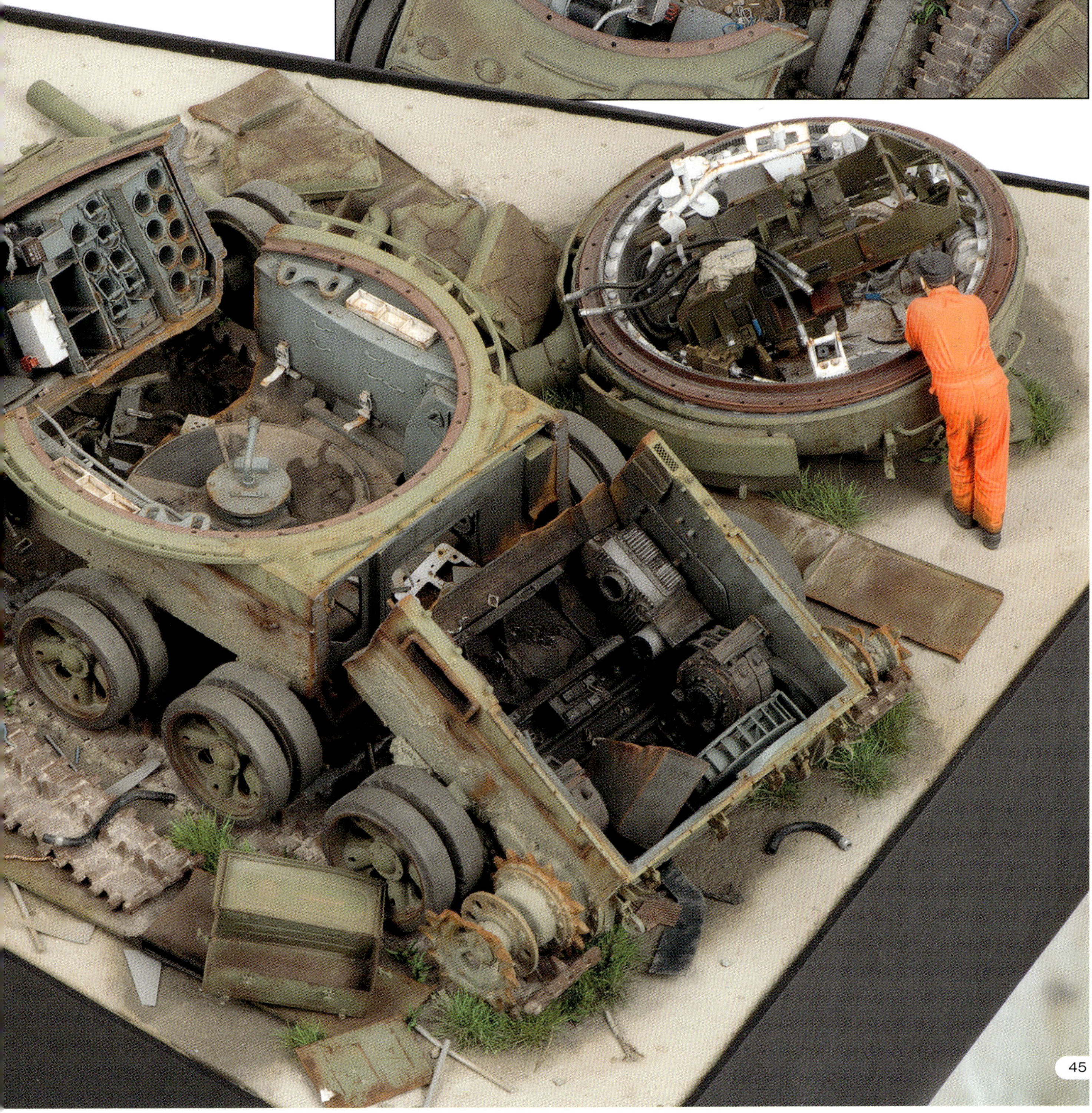

SCRAPYARD

Photos by Sergey Buyanov

These images are thought to be from Ussuriysk, Russia. They were the inspiration for the models in this book and we have tried to show a good cross section of the different vehicles and the differing condition of them in the hope that you will find them as interesting and inspiring as we did!

029

5

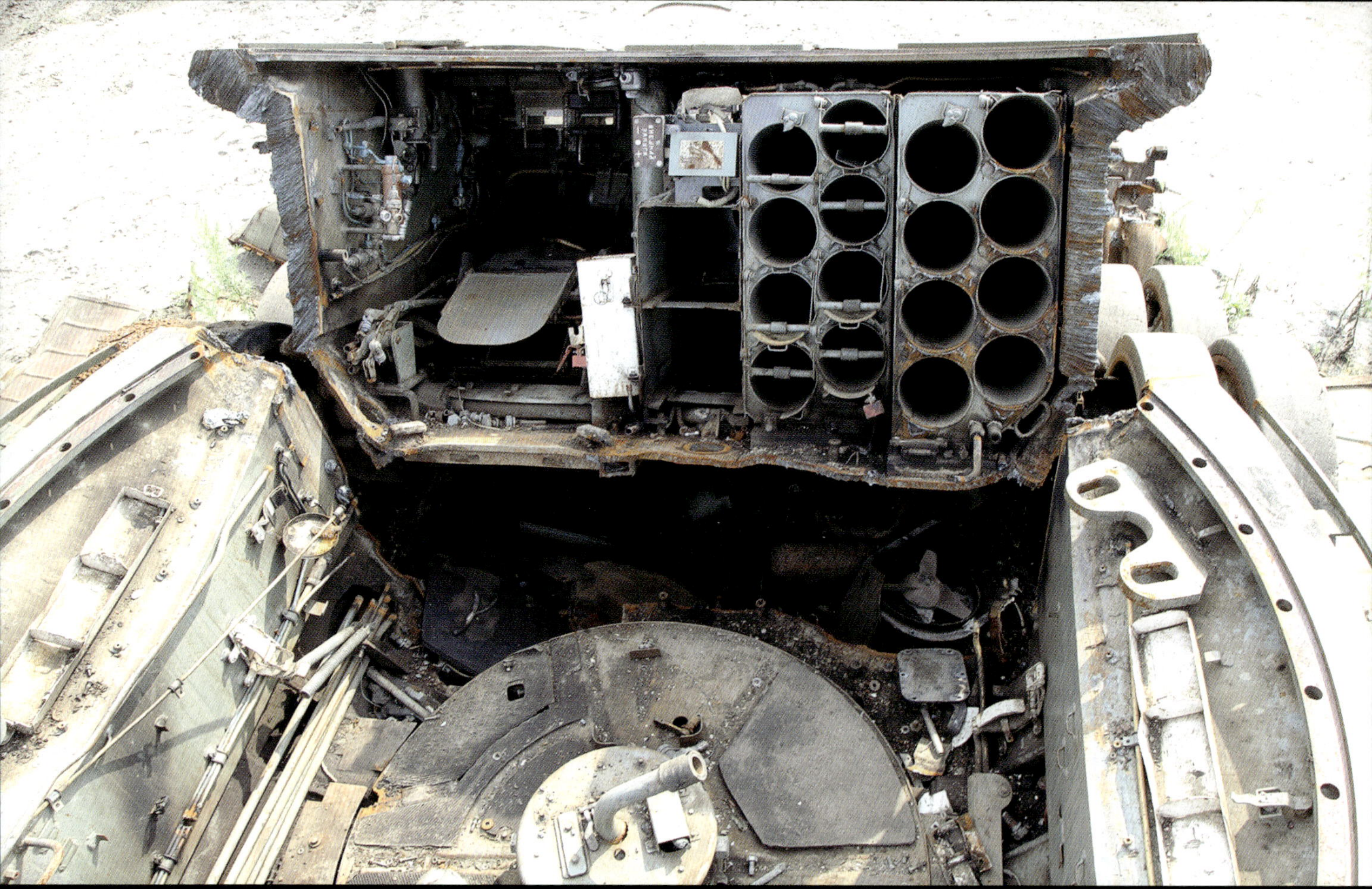

5

0.5

426
ЗИП

ЗИП

632

TO-55

GREEN AROUND THE GILLS

With many modelling projects there's a seemingly insignificant detail in a photograph that can catch the imagination and inspire us to start snipping at the sprues.

Whilst there are many worthy candidates in our scrapyard album, the daubed mint green emulsion (presumably to obscure some numerals or markings) really caught my eye and adds a punch of colour to this very poorly looking T-62. The excellent Trumpeter kit
T-62 BDD Model 1984 appeared a close match to the subject vehicle and would require little more than a few home made details. Rather than exactly replicating the subject vehicle I've gone out to render the textures, colours and level of disrepair before this aging warrior falls under the cutting torch.

Working to our reference photos I've left certain cannibalised items off the kit and detailed areas such as the fuel tank fittings and the open sighting unit. Thinning-out of some parts and replicating in foil others (front mudguard and exhaust deflector) are old-school tricks that cost nothing but time. The open sighting unit internals were scratchbuilt with plastic card and various rod and tube. The lack of tracks certainly saved time with this build! With the saved time I worked on the surface textures using Mr. Surfacer and Mr. Dissolved Putty using a stippling action and an old brush.

modelled by Mark Neville

GREEN AROUND THE GILLS

The first coat of colour was to emulate raw metal. A couple of colours from AK's German primer set were used applied in a pre-shade method with a tiny amount of silver added giving a faint metallic sheen. This coat was left a couple of days to fully cure bearing in mind the abuse to come!

Using both AK's 'Worn Effects' and 'Heavy Chipping' fluids would, in theory, give varying degrees of degraded paint surfaces. A coat of hairspray works in a similar way giving a semi-stable undercoat to the top colours.

I found brush application of the 'Heavy Chipping' fluid most successful. This was applied across thinner pressed metal parts such as the tool boxes and fuel tanks, a blast with a hair dryer speeds up the process.

The 'Worn Effects' fluid was applied through the airbrush, I found it a little thick and thinned it around 20% with acrylic thinners giving a wet, even application across the rest of the model.

Graugrun from AK came closest to the faded Russian green in my opinion from the colours I had to hand. With the dark brown undercoat acting as shadow colour the green was applied in various degrees of strength concentrating on the upper surfaces with a more intense colour. The finish at this stage isn't too important, there's many layers of colour to come.

Further fading and highlighting came from airbrushed Dunkelgelb in a random clouded pattern. The T-62 is beginning to take on some dimension now and the textures applied beginning to show. Where items have been stripped off the vehicle fittings were fabricated from scrap photoetch and stock rod and tube adding a touch of finesse.

The crumpled front mudguard was made by the old-school trick of burnishing foil onto the kit part creating an exact replica. A blunt cocktail stick and scalpel blade packet makes for a cheap upgrade.

This is the finished effect of the three initial layers of colours. The uneven application of the colours is important to not only add depth and dimension but also enhances the abandoned look of the faded, dead paint finish.

In hindsight I should have re-made the light guard (as David's) as the finished appearance, even after extensive thinning, is still too heavy.

Now for the fun part. With a few old worn-out brushes to hand and some clean, warm water the top surfaces were scrubbed away following the reference photos for the different degrees of damaged paint.

These processes (whether using specific products or hairspray) are best done soon after the application of the acrylic top colours to achieve successful and easy removal, certainly within an hour-or-so in my experiences. Allow yourself a good couple of hours for this process if the finish is all over a vehicle as this.

A cut-down brush that's past it's best works best on concentrated areas where very little paint remains. Cheap hogs hair brushes work well on larger areas. I found the AK Interactive products worked well together allowing good control of the effect.

The rear rubber mud guards have taken on a flat appearance as they're not attached to the missing side skirts, a simple job in plastic card. Brass tube was used for the stripped fittings. The bent and damaged mesh adds to the abandoned look.

Here you can see the difference between where the paint has been removed and the front is still yet to be done. Although I was working to the reference shots a little artistic licence comes into play. All is not lost if the top coats lift too much for your liking, simply re-apply some of your colour with a small piece of sponge to maintain the random speckled effect.

More vigorous work with the brush and water can allow the undercoat to bleed through a little, ideal for the effect I wanted to replicate on the heavy cheek armour.

A favourite colour of mine for replicating older rubber parts is Vallejo 'Black-Grey'. As the tyres would eventually have a heavy coating of dirt applied all that was needed was a quick brush painting.

The upper sections of the side skirts remained on the tank. I used the same colour to replicate the scratched and scuffed paint revealing the rubber, first with a very dry brush and then more deliberate fine lines.

I'd been looking forward to painting the areas of mint green on the turret! For the vibrance and opacity of colour I used some gouache of a reasonably thick consistency and chose a small flat brush to replicate the untidy strokes seen in the photographs.

Now it's time for colour filters and washes. I tend to work on a section at a time, first applying the filters and whilst the surface is still damp, a dark wash is applied with a fine spotter brush around the detail. The damp surface allows the wash to flow nicely. Many layers of filters, streaking and shadows culminate in a rich and varied surface.

I find a vehicle exposed to the elements as this one has been starts to exhibit an almost natural, organic look to the surface. Note the missing fuel cap on the fuel tank and the handle made from brass rod after removing the moulded-on kit part, all adding to the derelict feel.

Some strong tones of rust were added with pigment powder washed with fixing fluid. Once dried this can be burnished with a brush to produce subtle tones and highlights.

The brightest of Lifecolor's 'Rusty' diorama set's pigment powder was used sparingly on selected items. Thin sheet metal in the reference photographs shows brighter yellows and oranges, the exhaust shield an obvious candidate. The butterfly flap mechanism was built from scrap photoetch and brass rod, again, working from our scrapyard photographs.

Lifecolor's 'Reflecting Agent' powder was applied sparingly across some bare metal areas to give a subtle metallic effect. Soft pencil was used to highlight wear on edges and apply fine scratches. Note the very chalky finish to the faded paint on the rubber mudguards as in the photographs of the real vehicle.

Here's the accumulative effect of all of the techniques taking shape. The texture added by stippling Mr Surfacer looks effective on the fuel tanks.

Gun barrels usually tend to take on a slightly different finish due to the high quality of the materials used in manufacture. A polish with a mixture of the 'Burnt Rust' and 'Reflecting Agent' gave a pleasing finish. This method was also used on the cheek armour.

As the turret interior is bare I airbrushed several coats of flat black over this and the hull interior providing complete darkness to all the internals. As I planned to use pigment powders on the running gear and lower hull I worked the opposite way around to usual completing the upper surfaces first.

One of the final processes was an application of pigment powder mixed with fixing liquid. This dirty slurry was daubed on quite heavily and removed in places with a stiff brush. The leaking hubs were done with AK's 'Streaking Grime'.

It's important to blend a vehicle into the terrain it's sat on, something as heavy as a tank doesn't float across terrain. I've used some artistic licence with the earth colour using a more colourful tone than in the photographs, the warmth of the colour helps bring out the rust tones and faded green of the vehicle.

Any vehicle which hasn't moved in a such long time and is exposed to harsh elements will exhibit a lot of streaking as rain and moisture carries dirt and rust down the surfaces. Where water has pooled on raw metal the brighter orange rust tends to show.
Some localised light coloured washes of dust were applied in select areas.

With the tracks stripped off, some form of groundwork was essential to display the finished model and give the viewer no doubt about this retired warrior. Taking some of the elements from our album of photos a simple and quick display was constructed. A piece of 5mm foam-core board was cut to fit a simple frame. The same material was utilised for the rendered block wall, the paper surface was part stripped allowing the block-work to be scribed into the foam with a sharp hard pencil. The metal hoarding was made from thin aluminium plate with the ends folded in a photoetch clamp. The natural silver finish received several washes to age the appearance, the supporting posts are made from Evergreen 'H' beam styrene.

For convenience the earth texture was applied with a couple of coats of Tamiya Diorama Texture Paint (Powdered Snow) applied and 'pushed around' with a cheap brush. When dry the texture has a suitable fine grain to suit the dry earth. An airbrushed base coat was shaded and highlighted with dustings of pigment here and there to emphasise the dry surface. Vegetation was the final touch starting with tufts of summer grass from the Joefix range of diorama materials and have an excellent scale look and nice finesse. The taller plants are from natural mosses collected from the garden and dried out indoors. The sorry T-62 was set into the earth completing the scene. This kind of project is a great way to try out new products and techniques, with the wealth of 'magic potions' available on the market today much of the guess-work and trial and error is removed, add to this some quality colour reference shots and you've got some very enjoyable and satisfying hobby time.

GEORGIAN T-55

Modelled by Andy Taylor

As with all the models I build the key is finding the image that fuels your passion to recreate it in miniature. The series of photographs seen in this book are an example of the decaying Soviets wrecks that litter the site. The harsh effects of the weather can be clearly seen with all vehicles showing varying degrees of rust and decay. In particular this T-55M is in a state of disrepair and photographed at the Kharkov tank factory in the Ukraine, most of the zip boxes ,sights and fuel cells have already been removed.

GEORGIAN T-55

To enable me to build this model i had to hand a resin set from CMK that allows you to build a T-55AM, the parts included are for a Czech type which have a different engine deck arrangement sight that sits on top of the mantlet. New kits from Takom now allow the T-55 AM to be modelled without the need for conversion sets. As the model was to depict a very tired vehicle with lots of parts missing I opted to scratch build all the extra parts needed. The Tamiya kit was my only possible choice at the time although now numerous T-55 kits are now available from Takom and soon from Miniart.

512
928

GEORGIAN T-55

Assembly notes

Here we can see the extensive modifications to the base Tamiya kit which include the engine deck , extra armour plate on the glacis, completely reworked fenders. All these were constructed from Evergreen plastic card using various reference images in my library. Although not easily seen on the images the belly armour found on this type was also scratchbuilt according to images sourced from the internet and again relying on my own references.

The rear plate has the tow hooks taken from Trumpeters T-62 kit (the front road wheel with larger hub was also taken from the T-62 kit). The lane marker mount seen at the upper centre of the rear plate was constructed from plastic stock and detailed with weld beads from white Milliput.

Blast models supplied me with the M type loaders hatch, and commanders hatch lid, the bolted comb was taken from the old Esci T-55 which is probably the only part worth saving, grab handles were added again using brass wire for those

All the MG ammunition clips behind the smoke tubes were built using plastic strip and brass rod, i found the various etch ones on the market are quite poorly detailed.

The unditching beam brackets are from an old Verlinden T-55 etch set originally designed for the Esci T-55

The new belly armour seen in position.

The new scratchbuilt bow armour and just visible too, the belly armour. The excellent and highly accurate Modelkasten Rmsh track was used which sit perfectly on the chassis, in this case i wanted to show the idler wheel in a low un-tensioned position.

Right Wheels are cast by Steve Reid from a master I made to show the bearing detail, along with a Sprocket i mastered to allow the T-55 to carry the Rmsh track.

The sight unit in front of the Commander's hatch was scratchbuilt to show the missing internal details.

A new headlamp cage was made up from brass wire of around 0.7 diameter and added to the extra armour plate on the glacis along with other various brackets and fittings.

Various diameters of brass rod and tube from Albion alloys were used for the lighting conduits and bits of fuel lines that remained.

Main Barrel was the kit supplied one, which after careful assembly requires very little clean up, its more accurate than many of the turned metal ones available only surpassed by Aber.

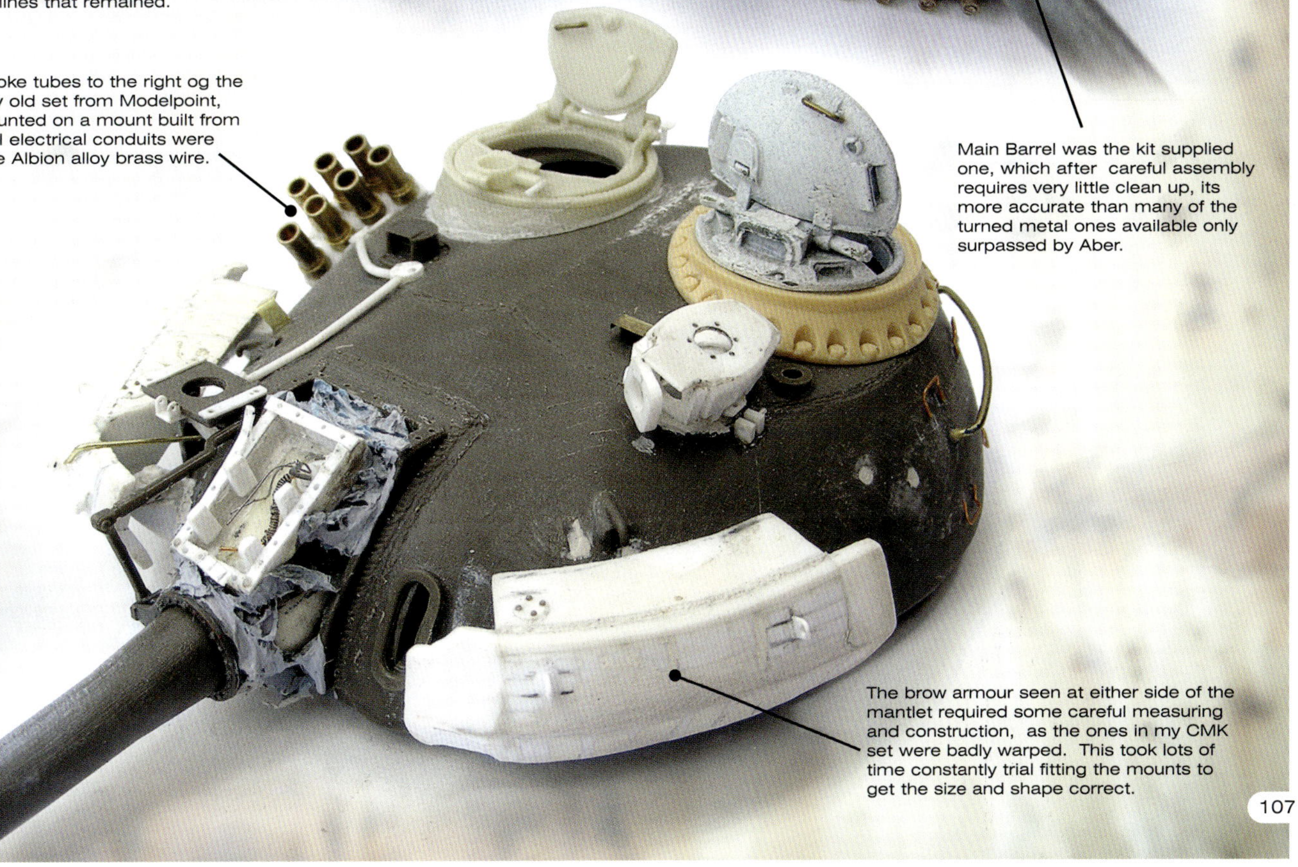

The Tuscha smoke tubes to the right og the turret are a very old set from Modelpoint, which were mounted on a mount built from plastic card. All electrical conduits were added using the Albion alloy brass wire.

The brow armour seen at either side of the mantlet required some careful measuring and construction, as the ones in my CMK set were badly warped. This took lots of time constantly trial fitting the mounts to get the size and shape correct.

The various tie down loops were replaced with copper wire examples and the big grab handle is made from brass rod.

Quite a lot of work went into the Mantlet area, to show the area under the missing range finder. A resin item from Mig productions supplied the bare mantlet, onto which i constructed the mounts for the unit. The area was further embellished with a ripped and torn cover often seen on abandoned T-54/55.

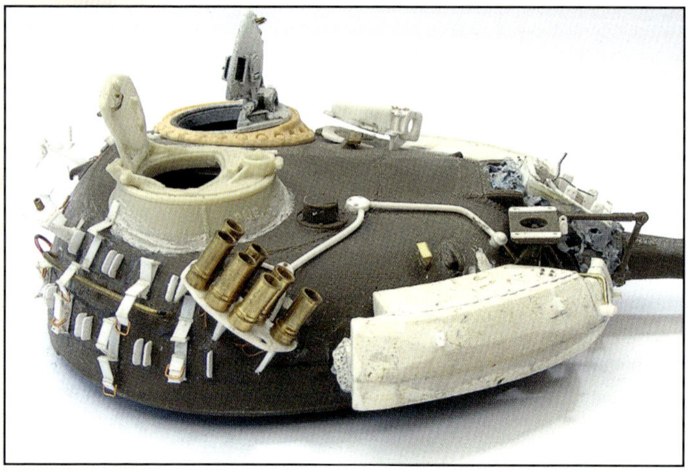

Fine copper wire is used to replicate the pieces of damaged electrical conduit.

Following my usual route of cleaning the model with warm soapy water to remove residues from sanding dust etc, I proceeded to apply a coat of Tamiya fine surface grey primer. It has excellent adhesion properties, and dries quickly to a satin finish.

First Colours

First steps were to add the various rust tones with the airbrush using brown Tamiya acrylics , the hairspray method was used to start the weathering process, here a mix of Tamiya olive green, dark yellow, yellow green and a touch of Linoleum brown were mixed to achieve the faded Soviet Green.

Weathering

After the various markings were applied freehand a simple process using thinned brown Humbrol colours to add a filter to the entire model was first added. While still wet, a heavier solution of Humbrol was employed to pin wash around details. Once left to dry overnight, some darker rust tones are sponged onto the larger areas of rust uncovered by the hairspray technique used earlier. A fine Winsor Newton brush was used to add darker rust tones to the smaller chips, concentrating in the centres.

Rust streaks were added using a ready mixed product from AK interactive, after leaving to dry for 10 minutes they are faded slightly by blending with a brush soaked in thinners. The rust streaking process was continued letting the previous streaks dry overnight by adding some burnt umber oil to the mix.

The wheels were treated in exactly the same manner as the rest of the vehicle, to great effect. Tracks were painted off the model to gain better access to the guide horns and track faces, a dark steel colour was applied first using Tamiya Nato Black, followed by various brown earth tones from Humbrol dry brushed on both faces. Various rust tones were also added as washes and left to dry. The final step was to add the earth and mud you can see gathered around details and compacted in the tracks.

512
928

512
928

The excellent mud splashes and dry earth effects from Ammo are invaluable for this effect, can be blended easily after letting set for 15 minutes, this was continued onto the tracks after thinning the mud consistency slightly to allow it to get into all the crevices.
Once allowed to dry, a final coat of lighter rust tones were dry brushed on to the track faces, guide horns , sprocket teeth and track contact area on the idler.

Although I have built many T-55 models this remains one of my favourite and most enjoyable projects to date. After attending Scale Model Challenge it was awarded a Gold medal which was a great surprise given the general high standard or work on display.
.